set apart

A PASSIONATE DEVOTION TO JESUS CHRIST

A FOUNDATIONAL STUDY IN CHRIST-CENTERED LIVING
FOR WOMEN OF ALL AGES

by Leslie Ludy

Set Apart: A Passionate Devotion to Jesus Christ (Workbook and Leader Guide)
Copyright © 2019 by Leslie Ludy & Set Apart Girl Ministries

All rights reserved. No part of this publication may be reproduced in any form unless it is in making copies for individual or groups who are taking the Set Apart course. You are not allowed to distribute, upload, resell, or reproduce this material for any other reason unless you receive prior written approval from Leslie Ludy & Set Apart Girl Ministries.

Published by Ellerslie Press, Windsor, Colorado

All Scripture quotations, unless otherwise noted, are taken from the New King James Version (NKJV) of the Bible. Public Domain. Bold and italic words in Scripture passages are for emphasis.

Cover Design by Annie Wesche,
Photography by iStock Photo
Printed in the United States of America.

Special thanks to Sarah Guthrie for her formative role in the creation of the Leader's Guide.

SetApartGirl.com

Table of Contents

Welcome Letter — 4

Week One: Set-Apartness Defined — 5

Week Two: Surrender – Daring to Lay Everything Down at Jesus' Feet — 11

Week Three: Freedom – Allowing the Gospel to Transform You from the Inside Out — 23

Week Four: Intimacy – Cultivating Daily, Passionate Communion with Christ — 35

Week Five: Devotion – Fixing Your Gaze Completely on Jesus — 49

Week Six: Radiance – Overcoming Insecurity through the Crucified Life — 59

Week Seven: Discretion – Adopting a Christ-Honoring Pattern for Digital Conduct — 69

Week Eight: Nobility – Honoring God and Others with Every Word Spoken — 79

Week Nine: Friendship – Becoming a Faithful "Friend of the Bridegroom" — 89

Week Ten: Discernment – Overcoming Deception through Godly Wisdom — 99

Week Eleven: Courage – Becoming Fearless for Such a Time as This — 109

Week Twelve: Love – Discovering the Power of a Poured-Out Life — 117

Appendix – Cleaning Out the Sanctuary — 125

Dear Friend,

Do you desire to *know* Jesus Christ deeply and intimately, as your dearest, closest, most trusted Friend? Do you long to not just talk about Him, sing about Him, and learn about Him, but to truly walk in daily, passionate relationship with Him? Are you tired of just reading about God's promises in the Bible and ready to *actually experience* the unmatched joy, peace that passes understanding, and soul-level satisfaction that is promised to those who follow Him?

If that is the kind of Christianity that you long for, this study is an invitation for you to come away with your Beloved. When you truly come away with Jesus, you won't focus on what you are giving up, but on what you are gaining. It is my prayer that this study will not only cast an inspiring and beautiful vision for biblical, Christ-centered, set-apart womanhood, but also to equip you to live it out. I'll be honest about the struggles and victories I've faced in my own pursuit to become a set apart woman, and share specific ways that God is continuing to refine me through the truths presented in this study.

My prayer is that this study will help you see Jesus more clearly and know Him more intimately. May it become a catalyst for God's refining fire to purify your heart and life, so that you can become a powerful instrument of change in the Body of Christ today.

Lord, send a revival, and let it begin in us!

Expectantly,

Leslie Ludy

Week One

Set-Apartness Defined

But know that the Lord has set apart the godly for Himself...
PSALM 4:3 NASB

An Invitation to Come Away with Jesus

My beloved spoke, and said to me,
"Rise up, my love, my fair one, and come away."
SONG OF SOLOMON 2:10

If we want to have unhindered fellowship with Jesus, we must be willing to come away from anything and everything standing in the way of wholehearted consecration to Him. Jesus stands ready to take your hand and lead you away from the empty pursuits of this world into the glorious realities of His Kingdom. He is inviting you to *"rise up and come away"* with Him. He desires to set you apart for His purposes and for His glory.

> Jesus says, 'Rise up, My love, My fair one and come away.' He asks you to come out from the world and be separate and touch not the unclean thing. Come altogether away from selfishness – from anything which would divide your chaste and pure love to Christ – your soul's Husband. Come away from your old habits. Leave all these things. Come away to private communion. Come away, shut the doors of your chamber and talk with your Lord Jesus and have close and intimate dealing with Him ... Come altogether away from the world, by making your dedication to Christ perfect, complete, unreserved, sincere, spotless.[1]
>
> Charles Spurgeon

What Leads to True Set-Apartness? Pursuing Christ Above All Else.

Jeremiah 29:13 says, "…you will seek Me and find Me, when you search for Me with *all* your heart" (emphasis added). When our desire for Christ becomes so great that we begin to seek Him as if we are searching for priceless treasure, when we are willing to give up all the treasures of this world in order to gain Him — that is when He will draw nearer to us than we ever imagined possible. (See Psalm 119:72, Matthew 13:46, and Philippians 3:8.)

What Makes the Set Apart Life Possible?

When we try to achieve a set apart life on our own merit and in our own strength, we will find ourselves on the fast track to legalism. It is only possible by leaning on God's enabling grace. God's grace equips us to live the set apart life to which He has called us.

Does Set-Apartness Mean Perfection?

Certainly not — but it means total surrender to the One who *is* Perfect. It means letting Him have His way in us and holding nothing back from Him; removing anything that would stand in the way of our ability to love Him with all our heart, soul, mind, and strength.

> Comrades in this solemn fight, let us settle it as something that cannot be shaken: we are here to live holy, loving, lowly lives. We cannot do this unless we walk very, very close to our Lord Jesus. Anything that would hinder us from the closest walk possible, till we see Him face-to-face, is not for us.[2]
>
> Amy Carmichael

THIS WEEK

Read Psalm 45:10-11:

Listen, O daughter,
Consider and incline your ear;
Forget your own people also, and your father's house;
So the King will greatly desire your beauty;
Because He is your Lord, worship Him.

Reflect: Do I sense Christ calling me to come away with Him? Am I willing to pursue Him above all else, to serve Him without holding back, and offer myself completely to Him without reserve? (If so, take some time to write your prayer of commitment to Him).

_____
_____
_____
_____
_____
_____
_____
_____
_____

Read John 15:16:

You did not choose Me, but I chose you and appointed you that you should go and bear fruit, and that your fruit should remain…

Reflect: Knowing that Jesus has chosen me and appointed me to bear fruit for His glory, how should this affect my decisions on a daily basis?

Soul-Searching Questions:

Am I willing to come away with Jesus?

Do I understand what I will be leaving behind as a result? What do I have to consciously cut off in order to follow after Christ with all that I am?

Is there anything I am hesitating to leave behind in order to follow Him completely?

Am I willing to let go of worldly pursuits and applause to be set apart for Him?

Have I been seeking to live set apart for Him in my own strength? Am I willing to lean on His enabling power instead of my own determination?

_____

_____

_____

_____

Have I been seeking Christ with all my heart, or has my heart been divided? What changes do I need to make in my life in order to seek Him with my whole heart?

_____

_____

_____

_____

Take it Deeper

The following resources have been selected to enhance your journey through this lesson and take these truths deeper into your heart.

Watch *He Is* — a short film available at Ellerslie.com.
Q. Meditating on all that Christ is, are you motivated to become passionately devoted to Him? Which names of God most stood out to you? Why?

_____

_____

_____

_____

Watch *Many Beautiful Things* — a documentary about the life of Lilias Trotter (available on iTunes and Amazon Prime Video).
Q. How did Lilias's life reflect the principle of "coming away with Jesus"? What inspires you about her example of radical givenness to Jesus?

_____

_____

_____

_____

Surrender — Daring to Lay Everything Down at Jesus' Feet

*..."If anyone desires to come after Me, let him deny himself,
and take up his cross, and follow Me."*
MATTHEW 16:24

..."whoever of you does not forsake all that he has cannot be My disciple."
LUKE 14:33

The Foundation of the Set Apart Life is Surrender

Imagine your soul as a home. We may prefer to keep Christ in the hallway, or only allow Him into certain rooms of our soul, but if you feel Christ knocking on the door of your heart, be willing to let Him in. And not just into the hallway, but into *every single room* within your soul. No matter what He asks, He is worthy of our wholehearted *yes!*

Giving God the Pen

Your life is a story written by God Himself. However, the flesh can quickly take control of the pen of our lives. Instead of attempting to craft your own plans and purposes, surrender the pen of your entire life to God to script as He sees fit. His plans may be different from yours, but they will be infinitely better and more fulfilling!

*Delight yourself also in the LORD,
and He shall give you the desires of your heart.*
PSALM 37:4

A Prayer of Surrender

My Lord, I have mistreated You all my life. I have treated You like a servant. When I wanted You, I called for You; when I was about to engage in something important I beckoned You to come and help me perform my task. I have sought to use You only as a servant to help me in my self-appointed work. I will do so no more. Lord, I give You this body of mine; from my head to my feet, I give it to You. My hands, my limbs, my eyes, my brain; all that I am inside and out, I hand over to You. Live in and through me whatever life You please. You may send this body to Africa, or lay it on a bed with cancer. You may blind my eyes, or send me with Your message to Tibet. You may take this body to the Eskimos, or send it to a hospital with pneumonia. This body of mine is Yours alone from this moment on.[1]

WALTER WILSON

Is Our God Trustworthy?

He who did not spare His own Son, but delivered Him up for us all, how shall He not with Him also freely give us all things?
ROMANS 8:32

…casting all your care upon Him, for He cares for you.
1 PETER 5:7

Greater love has no one than this, than to lay down one's life for his friends. You are My friends…
JOHN 15:13-14A

I went away alone to a cave in a mountain called Arima, in Japan. I felt many feelings of fear about the future. That's why I was there. I wanted to be alone with God. The devil kept on whispering, "It's all right now, but what about afterwards? You are going to be very lonely." And he painted pictures of loneliness. I can see them still. Then I turned to my God in a kind of desperation and said, "Lord, what can I do? And He said, "None of them that trust in Me shall be desolate" (Ps. 34:22). That word has been with me ever since. It has been fulfilled to me. It will be fulfilled to you. Only live for Him who redeemed you and trust Him to take care of you – and He will.[2]

Amy Carmichael

Remember, surrender is a daily process – not a one-time experience.

Four Keys to a Surrendered Heart

1. Know Who You Are Surrendering To

A glimpse of who Jesus is and who He wants to be in our lives:

>My Portion, My Maker, My Husband (Isaiah 54:5)
>
>My Well-Beloved (Song of Solomon 1:13)
>
>My Savior (2 Peter 3:18)
>
>My Hope (1 Timothy 1:1)
>
>My Brother (Mark 3:35)
>
>My Helper (Hebrews 13:6)
>
>My Physician (Jeremiah 8:22)
>
>My Healer (Luke 9:11)
>
>My Refiner (Malachi 3:3)
>
>My Purifier (Malachi 3:3)
>
>My Lord, Master (John 13:13)
>
>My Servant (Luke 12:37)
>
>My Example (John 13:15)
>
>My Teacher (John 3:2)
>
>My Shepherd (Psalm 23:1)

My Keeper (John 17:12)

My Feeder (Ezekiel 34:23)

My Leader (Isaiah 40:11)

My Restorer (Psalm 23:3)

My Resting Place (Jeremiah 50:6)

My Meat (John 6:55)

My Drink (John 6:55)

My Passover (1 Corinthians 5:7)

My Peace (Ephesians 2:14)

My Wisdom (1 Corinthians 1:30)

My Righteousness (1 Corinthians 1:30)

My Sanctification (1 Corinthians 1:30)

My Redemption (1 Corinthians 1:30)

My All in All (Colossians 3:11)

Let the things of earth grow strangely dim in the light of His glory and grace!

2. Trust His Timing

Read the story of Abraham attempting to rush ahead of God in Genesis 16:1-17:19. In contrast, what happens when we try to script our own story out of impatience? What happens when we leave the pen entirely in God's hands?

3. Embrace the Crucified Life

Our culture promotes a self-centered attitude: *What do I want? What will make me happy?*

Christ's reasoning is very different: "…if anyone would come after Me, let Him **deny Himself, and take up His Cross and follow Me**" (Matt. 16:24, emphasis added).

WEEK 2: SURRENDER

This is what it means to embrace the crucified life – to take up our cross, deny self, and follow Him.

> Father, let me loose my clutch on everything temporal. My life, my reputation, my possessions, Lord, let me loose the tension of the grasping hand. Open my hand to receive the nail of Calvary, as Christ's was opened. He thought Heaven, yea, equality with God, not a thing to be clutched at. So let me release my grasp.[3]
>
> Jim Elliot

> Lord, I'm going to love and obey and serve You not because of anything I will get out of it – but I'm going to love and obey and serve simply because You are worthy, and I'm not trying to make a deal with You.[4]
>
> Paris Reidhead

4. Lay Down Idols

> *No one can serve two masters; for either he will hate the one and love the other, or else he will be loyal to the one and despise the other…*
> MATTHEW 6:24
>
> *I am the LORD; that is My name! I will not yield My glory to another or My praise to idols.*
> ISAIAH 42:8 NIV
>
> *…For it is written, "You shall worship the LORD your God, and Him only you shall serve."*
> LUKE 4:8B
>
> *…give me an undivided heart, that I may fear Your name.*
> PSALM 86:11B

Identifying Our Idols

Removing anything that takes a higher position than Jesus Christ

Idolatry divides our heart from Christ. When we have idolatry in our life, we may say (or even believe) that Jesus Christ has our whole heart, but in reality we place our hopes and affections in pursuits outside of Him (health, money, romance, and so on). Scripture is clear: When we become slaves to our appetites, our heath or financial goals, our romantic pursuits, our popularity, our comforts, or anything else, we cannot be the servants of Christ.

How often do we stand in a worship service and sing songs like, "You are my All in All" while our minds are preoccupied with thoughts of a relationship or a career opportunity? How often is our identity far more wrapped up in our popularity, achievements, or possessions than in the simple, glorious reality that we are daughters of the King? How often do we think, *If I could only (get married, make more money, lose weight, have more friends, do something exciting, and so on) THEN I would be happy, and I would make Jesus my number one focus*? We ask God to give us the desires of our heart, all the while forgetting that *He* should always be the chief desire of our heart.

How to Identify an Idol in Your Life

1) **You can't imagine giving it up.** You think: *If I don't eat health food, I'll surely die an early death*; or *If I can't listen to my favorite music everyday, I'll be miserable and depressed*; or *If I don't get married, life won't be worth living.*

2) **You spend more time and energy on that area than you do on your relationship with Christ.** For instance, maybe you spend eight hours each week on movies or social media, but only ten minutes in prayer or in studying God's Word. Or maybe you invest the majority of your time and energy into a relationship (or the pursuit of one) and have little time left over to seek Christ or share Him with others. As much as we don't like to admit it, the areas that claim the majority of our spare time are those that have the biggest hold upon our hearts.

3) **You find more delight and happiness in that area of your life than you do in your relationship with Christ.** It's not wrong if earthly things bring us a certain level of comfort or happiness. But Jesus must always remain our source of deepest satisfaction. A great way to determine whether you are finding your fulfillment in Christ is to ask yourself this question: *If this area of my life was suddenly stripped away from me, would Jesus be enough?*

Countless Christians throughout the ages (and today in persecuted countries around the world) have made astounding personal sacrifices, even giving up their very lives, in order to put Jesus first. If these men and women are willing to give up everything in order to serve only one Master, Jesus Christ, can we not do the same? If we are not cultivating an undivided heart toward Christ right now in areas such as food, money, and romance, how can we expect to keep our gaze fixed upon Him when greater trials and sufferings come?

Key Areas to Prayerfully Surrender

1) Future hopes and dreams
2) Romantic relationships, marriage, and family
3) Reputation and popularity
4) Material possessions
5) Pop-culture entertainment
6) Our very lives!

…from all your idols, will I cleanse you.
EZEKIEL 36:25 KJV

THIS WEEK

Read Romans 8:32:

He that spared not His own Son, but delivered Him up for us all, how shall He not with Him also freely give us all things?

Reflect: Am I ready to lay my life completely at the feet of Jesus and dare to trust Him with my future? Am I actively seeking to know the One I am surrendering to? Why would I ever hesitate to trust the One who gave His very life to rescue me?

Read Psalm 51:10:

Create in me a clean heart, O God, and renew a steadfast spirit within me.

Reflect: Am I willing for God's Spirit to shine His searchlight within my soul? What do I sense has become an area of idolatry in my life? What can I do this week that will ensure I devote time to getting alone with Jesus to place anything on the altar that has taken a wrong place in my life?

Soul-Searching Questions:

Using page 17 as a reference, set aside time to prayerfully examine each area of your life to determine if idolatry has crept in, or if each area remains under the care and keeping of Christ. The questions below can also assist you in your search. As God lovingly brings things to mind, respond in obedience by re-committing those areas back to God through prayer.

Am I clinging to my own "rights" or my own agenda in any area of my life?

_____

_____

_____

_____

Are there habits, activities, things, relationships in my life that I cannot imagine giving up? What is God leading me to do with each of these things?

Is there any area of my life that brings me more delight, happiness, and refreshment than is found in my walk with Christ?

Am I willing to place the "pen of my life" entirely in Christ's hands?

What, if anything, do I need to change in my life so that He can be in total control?

Do I sincerely and completely trust God with my future?

_____

_____

_____

_____

_____

Take it Deeper

The following resources have been selected to enhance your journey through this lesson and take these truths deeper into your heart.

Listen to *Identifying Idols* – an episode of the Set Apart Girl weekly podcast available at SetApartGirl.com.
Q. Continue to allow Jesus Christ to press you in areas that have become marked by idolatry rather than true worship of Him. Consider: *What is Jesus asking me to place on the altar today?*

Listen to *Ten Shekels and a Shirt* – a classic sermon by Paris Reidhead available at SermonIndex.net.
Q. Am I living for my own happiness or for the glory of God? Is there anything God is speaking to my heart through this message?

If you desire to go through a spiritual house-cleaning process, consider setting aside time to go through the "Cleaning Out the Sanctuary" tool located on page 125 of this guide.

Freedom — Allowing the Gospel to Transform You from the Inside Out

For by grace you have been saved through faith, and that not of yourselves; it is the gift of God…
EPHESIANS 2:8

Stand fast therefore in the liberty by which Christ has made us free, and do not be entangled again with a yoke of bondage.
GALATIANS 5:1

Is Victory Over Sin Possible?

Many Christians have come to the conclusion that the epic visions of triumph and victory presented in Scripture are nothing more than poetic-sounding, larger-than-life ideals — sort of like those inspirational posters we see at the doctor's office or gym. We may be mentally motivated or emotionally moved by the beautiful promises and righteous standards presented in the Bible, but not many of us expect to live them out in everyday life — at least not on a consistent basis.

But God does not give us instructions that He won't enable us to carry out. If He said it, and He cannot lie, then what more is there to argue or discuss? Our God doesn't tease us by making promises to us that He doesn't intend to fulfill. (See Numbers 23:19.)

Why is there such a big gap between the power of the Cross and the majesty of the Gospel as presented in Scripture, and the oft-mediocre reality of our daily lives?

The answer is simple: We have lost our understanding of the enabling power of God. The message of the Cross is much more than simply knowing and believing the truth. It also means being supernaturally equipped by God's enabling grace to live a victorious life that would otherwise be impossible.

> God does not give us instructions that He won't enable us to carry out.[1]
>
> **Elisabeth Elliot**

Grace is not merely the "hug of God," but the enabling power to live out the impossible life He has called us to.

> Obedience to God is always possible. It is a deadly error to fall into the notion that when feelings are extremely strong we can do nothing but act on them.[2]
>
> **Elisabeth Elliot**

> Do not give way to lowness when you are young. Rise up on the strength of God and resolve to conquer.[3]
>
> **Catherine Booth**

> When I try, I fail. When I trust, He succeeds![4]
>
> **Corrie ten Boom**

Reckoning Truth – Declaring His Word to be Your Reality

> *Likewise you also, reckon yourselves to be dead indeed to sin,*
> *but alive to God in Christ Jesus our Lord.*
> **ROMANS 6:11**

It is not about your past experience or your feelings, but about His unchanging Word. If He said it and He cannot lie, you can reckon it as true.

WEEK 3: FREEDOM

Seven Keys to Spiritual Freedom

1. Repent and Turn

In order to truly become a "new creation in Christ" we must first pass from death to life. (See John 5:24 and 2 Corinthians 5:17.) Old things must pass away. We must reckon our "old self" crucified in Christ and let the life of Christ live and reign within our soul. Becoming "dead to self" and "alive to Christ" is what the Gospel is all about.

In a nutshell, repentance is the process of recognizing when we have been heading in the wrong direction, acknowledging our failure, asking God to forgive us of our sin, and then – by His enabling grace – turning to walk in the opposite direction.

If you are unsure whether God has truly forgiven you, it's possible that you haven't had a clear understanding of true repentance, or the power of "Christ in you, the hope of glory" (Col. 1:27). I would encourage you to spend time in the presence of God – let Him shine His searchlight into your soul, convict you of sin, wash you clean by the power of Jesus' blood, and give you the enabling grace to repent and turn from your sin. Remain in the presence of God until you have been made a new creation in Christ. Let Him overtake you from the inside out. Surrender your entire life into His hands, and let His power overtake you and equip you to live a life you could never live on your own.

Repentance is so much more than just saying you are sorry for past sins. It's about living a completely different lifestyle and having a completely different attitude – through the power of Christ in you. Settle it in your heart that your life is no longer your own, you have been bought with a price – the precious blood of Christ. Remember that when you come to Christ, you are making a sacred covenant exchange; all that you are for all that He is. When your old self has died with Christ and you have become a new creation in Him, you have the power to repent and turn from your sin and live a life of righteousness that you could never live on your own.

True repentance brings about a true life change.

2. Embrace Conviction, Reject Condemnation

Conviction and condemnation are very different, however it can be confusing which "voice" we are hearing in our daily lives. In order to distinguish whether you are feeling convicted by God's Spirit or condemned by the enemy of your soul, it is important to be trained to understand what spirit conviction and condemnation are each rooted in, and what they produce in our lives.

Conviction is the gentle prick of discomfort upon our soul from the Spirit of God when we feel something needs to be corrected within us – for example, sinful attitudes and actions that His Spirit desires to cleanse from our lives. Conviction is a sign of God's love towards us and is always paired with hope. In fact, you can welcome it as an invitation to be made more like Jesus Christ and as a gateway to enter into deeper fellowship with Him.

Condemnation, on the other hand, is rooted in despair and hopelessness; it has no life associated with it. It gives the message that you are a failure. The voice of condemnation questions God's love, leads us to doubt, keeps our eyes focused on our faults, and is a deliberate tactic of the enemy to seek to overthrow our faith and keep us from moving forward in victory in our lives.

Don't allow the enemy's condemnation to drown out the sweet sense of God's conviction in your inner life. When you hear the voice of accusation whispering to your soul, refuse to listen or give it any credibility in your soul. Those messages never come from God.

Embrace true conviction as a gift from your loving Heavenly Father who desires deeper intimacy with you, with the intent to shape you to be a set apart woman who reflects the beauty of Heaven. As you respond wholeheartedly to conviction, it will lead to amazing life and freedom in Christ.

3. Make Things Right

Oftentimes, when God brings conviction into our lives, He asks us to go beyond merely saying a prayer of repentance. He may lead us to take specific steps in order to make things right with others. Even if it is hard to go to someone you have wronged and make something right, there are amazing spiritual benefits that come from those humbling steps of obedience.

In whatever ways God may lead you to make things right, again, the key is to respond with wholehearted obedience in order to experience lasting freedom over sin.

4. Agree with God

Proverbs 3:5 tells us, "Trust in the Lord with all your heart, and **do not lean on your own understanding**" (ESV, emphasis added). When it comes to receiving God's forgiveness we all too often try to lean on our own understanding rather than standing firmly on the promises of God. Our own mind and emotions – or even "common sense" – may tell us that we can never truly be free from our past sins. But what does God's Word say about it?

He says, "Therefore, if anyone is in Christ, he is a new creation; **old things have passed away**; behold, all things have become new" (2 Cor. 5:17, emphasis added).

He says, "If we confess our sins, He is faithful and just to **forgive us our sins** and to cleanse us from all unrighteousness" (1 Jn. 1:9, emphasis added).

He says, "Purge me with hyssop, and **I shall be clean**; wash me, and I shall be whiter than snow" (Ps. 51:7, emphasis added).

He says, "As far as the east is from the west, **so far has He removed** our transgressions from us" (Ps. 103:12, emphasis added).

The only way to truly walk in the amazing reality of God's forgiveness is to stop listening to our own human perspective and start agreeing with God. His Word reminds us, "…let God be true, but every man a liar…" (Rom. 3:4). In other words, *the only opinion that truly matters is His*. One of the best ways to start agreeing with God that your past sins are truly forgiven is to memorize a few key Scriptures on forgiveness and meditate on them often, especially when you are tempted to give in to guilt, shame, remorse, and doubt. If we ask God for the enabling grace to say *no* to guilt and doubt, and *yes* to the promises in His Word, He will give us everything that we need to agree with Him.

We must bring our sin to the feet of Jesus, acknowledge what He has done for us, and pour out our love and gratitude upon Him. By His grace, may we choose to, "Stand fast … in the liberty by which **Christ has made us free**, and not be entangled again with a yoke of bondage" (Gal. 5:1, emphasis added).

Overcoming Shame Through the Power of the Cross

So many of us – though we have confessed and repented of our past sins – are not truly walking in the freedom that Christ purchased for us on the Cross. Our own emotions, or the enemy of our soul, often convince us that those sins will always haunt us, and always weigh us down. Many women have said to me, "I know that God can forgive me, but I just can't *forgive myself*." What that statement really means is, "I just can't seem to agree with God that I am forgiven."

In reality, God hasn't asked us to "forgive ourselves." *He* is the Forgiver – we are the *recipients* of His forgiveness. Our job isn't to "let ourselves off the hook" for past sins. Rather, our job is to *believe what He says*. It sounds so simple, yet this is where many of us get tripped up. We try to punish ourselves for past sins, forgetting that Christ already bore our punishment on the Cross. When we repent and turn, He forgives us and sets us free from the past – and not just partially free – but *free indeed!*

If you have been weighed down with regret and guilt over past sins, yet you have repented and asked to be made new, then God wants to show you that your prison door is unlocked. You don't need to stay in that prison anymore. All you need to do is rise up, push against the iron bars, and discover that they swing wide open. You have been set free by His blood. Now, you need to walk in that reality.

5. Take Back the Enemy's Ground

If you have allowed habitual sin to remain in your life or have never truly repented of past sins, then it's likely that the enemy has gained some territory in your inner life. If you have let sin control you, then the enemy has gained a "legal right" to harass you — wreaking havoc in your spiritual life and plaguing you with doubt, fear, anger, guilt, etc. When you repent of past sins and allow Christ to wash you clean, it's crucial to take back the territory that you have previously given to the enemy.

Let God reveal to you any area in which Satan has gotten a hold in your life. Once you repent and are made new in that area, tell the enemy that he must go, and spiritually take back any ground that he has claimed. Then, if he tries to harass you with guilt, shame, remorse, or temptation toward those old habits, remind him that this territory now belongs to God and stand firmly upon promises such as: "…greater is He who is in me than he who is in the world" (1 Jn. 4:4 NASB). Don't allow the enemy to push you around or weigh you down with past sins that have already been covered by the blood of Jesus. When you are in Christ and Christ is in you, you have the power to resist the enemy, and when you do, he *must* flee. (See James 4:7.)

6. Know the Power of Christ in You

Coming to the Cross means much more than believing that Christ died for your sins. It means exchanging all that you are for all that He is. It means being overtaken by His divine indwelling power, which supernaturally equips you to live a holy, triumphant life that would be impossible on your own. When you grasp the mystery of "Christ in you, the hope of glory" (Col. 1:27), you will grasp the secret to set apart living.

> Think what it is we really possess, if Christ is in us … all power, all grace, all purity, and all fullness, absolutely everything to make all grace abound toward us, in us, and through us, are stored up in Him who verily dwells within us.[5]
>
> Evan Hopkins

Many believers have resigned themselves to the attitude, "I'll always struggle with sin; I shouldn't expect victory this side of Heaven." We read Paul's statement in Romans 7, "O wretched man that I am! Who will save me from this body of death?" (v.24) and reason, *Well, if Paul couldn't overcome sin, who am I to think I'm any different*? But the answer to Paul's question is presented clearly in the next sentence. "Thanks be to **God** through **Jesus Christ our Lord**!" (Rom. 7:25 ESV, emphasis added). Because of the work of the Cross and the enabling grace of Christ that dwells within us, we have the power to "reckon ourselves to be dead indeed to sin, but alive to God in Christ Jesus our Lord" (Rom. 6:11). Our "old man" has been crucified with Christ. (See Romans 6:6.) Therefore, we are free to no longer serve sin, but to walk in the light, as He is in the light. (See 1 John 1:7.)

Embracing the enabling grace of God to overcome sinful strongholds does not mean living in "sinless perfection" and never stumbling again. (See Philippians 3:12.) But neither should we expect to be controlled by the bondage of sin or legalism. Let us no longer underestimate the power of the Cross or doubt God's willingness and ability to transform us into *"new creations"* in Christ! (See 2 Corinthians 5:17.)

> It is more humbling for us to take what grace offers, than to bewail our wants and worthlessness.[6]
>
> Andrew Bonar

7. Know Your Position

There is therefore now no condemnation to those who are in Christ Jesus, who do not walk according to the flesh, but according to the Spirit.
ROMANS 8:1

The Bible says that all things are under the feet of Jesus Christ – if something cannot get to Him (i.e. sin, fear, pride), then it cannot get to you.

THIS WEEK

Read Galatians 5:1:

Stand fast ... in the liberty by which Christ has made us free, and do not be entangled again with a yoke of bondage.

Reflect: Am I walking in the freedom of soul that Christ purchased for me on the Cross? Am I calling myself a Christian while still living in bondage to sin and self-effort? Am I ready to fully embrace the power of the Cross to transform my life and set me free from any bondage?

Read Titus 1:2 (emphasis added):

*...in hope of eternal life which God, **who cannot lie**, promised before time began...*

Reflect: Do I believe that God can lie? If God said it, can it be anything but true? Am I willing to start agreeing with God and tuning out the voice of my own emotions and experience?

As mentioned in week two's *Take it Deeper* section, if you desire to go through a spiritual house-cleaning process, consider setting aside time to go through the "Cleaning Out the Sanctuary" tool located on page 125 of this guide.

Soul-Searching Questions

Do I understand the power of *Christ in me*? Am I desirous to let Him enable me to live the impossible life of victory to which I am called?

_____

_____

_____

_____

Am I *in Christ*? If I am *in Christ,* and all things are under His feet, what does that mean for me when it comes to sin, doubt, and defeat?

What promises of God do I need to reckon true, whether I feel they are true or not?

Am I ready to "reckon myself dead indeed to sin" by the enabling power of God?

Have I confessed areas of known sin to God and repented? If so, do I agree with Him that He has removed my sin as far away as the east is from the west?

Do I need to take back any ground from the enemy? Are there areas of my life that need to be reclaimed and placed under the authority of Jesus Christ?

Are there things in my past that need to be confessed and made right?

Am I tuning into the voice of God's conviction or am I listening to Satan's condemnation?

Take it Deeper

The following resources have been selected to enhance your journey through this lesson and take these truths deeper into your heart.

Watch or listen to *In Christ* – a sermon by Eric Ludy available at Ellerslie.com.
Q. Are there specific steps I need to take in order to "reckon" God's truth in my life? Do I truly understand that I am now in Christ? How should that reality change my life?

Watch *The Gospel* – a short film available at Ellerslie.com. Let God speak to your heart about how His glorious Good News should impact you every moment of every day.

Listen to *The Spirit of the Humble* – a sermon by Eric Ludy available at Ellerslie.com.
Q. Are there specific things God is convicting me to make right in my life? Are there people I need to reconcile with? What are the practical steps I sense He is asking me to take?

Intimacy – Cultivating Daily, Passionate Communion with Christ

And you will seek Me and find Me,
*when you search for Me with **all** your heart.*
JEREMIAH 29:13, EMPHASIS ADDED

Key Question:

What is the secret to daily, intimate fellowship with Jesus?

The man who would know God must give time to Him.[1]

A. W. Tozer

Are You Too Busy to Pray?

Jesus tells us, "Blessed are those servants whom the master, when he comes, will find watching…" (Lk. 12:37). The word "watching" in this context literally means *to be roused from sleep, to be awake, to be on the alert.*

Most of us desire to know God more than we already do. We sense our need for more of His presence and power in our daily lives. We feel an aching spiritual hunger in our souls for something more in our relationship with Him. And yet, we often balk at doing the one thing that would bring us closer to Him – spending time in His presence.

The Bible offers a practical solution for growing closer to God: "Draw near to God and He will draw near to you…" (Jms. 4:8). Are we willing to do whatever it takes to draw near to Jesus? Are we willing to lose sleep, food, productivity, social status, and "down time" in order to make time with God the highest priority of our life? Do we have a spiritual determination that says, "No obstacle will keep me from my King — even if I must go up to the rooftop and break through the house tiles to get to Him" — just as the lame man's friends did in order to get to Jesus? (See Mark 2:4.)

> … "A certain man gave a great supper and invited many, and sent his servant at supper time to say to those who were invited, 'Come, for all things are now ready.' But they all with one accord began to make excuses. The first said to him, 'I have bought a piece of ground, and I must go and see it. I ask you to have me excused.' And another said, 'I have bought five yoke of oxen, and I am going to test them. I ask you to have me excused.' Still another said, 'I have married a wife, and therefore I cannot come.'"
>
> LUKE 14:16-20

Our King has prepared an amazing feast for us. He desires to fill us with His very life and satisfy the deepest needs within our souls. He does not invite us to His banquet demandingly, but lovingly and longingly. He sacrificed His life and shed His blood so that He could be in relationship with us. And He stands at the table, eagerly waiting to commune with us. We have the amazing, astounding, thrilling privilege of being invited daily into the presence of the King of all kings, to come before His throne of grace, and to partake of all that He is. Yet how often do we say, "I cannot come; I have something more important to do. I ask You to have me excused."? What a heartbreaking response! It's as if someone is offering us a handful of diamonds, and we choose a pile of pebbles instead.

Cultivating Daily Intimacy with Christ

It is only when we choose to live by the "too busy NOT to pray" principle that will we experience a thriving walk with Christ and, thusly, a life that really works.

1. Don't Let Emotions Lead

> Don't pray when you feel like it.
> Have an appointment with the Lord, and keep it![2]
>
> **Corrie ten Boom**

Daily life is filled with hundreds of choices to either give in to our selfish whims or yield to Christ's Spirit and obey His commands. For example, when the alarm goes off in the morning, do you yield to the beckoning whisper of Christ's Spirit, asking you to get up and spend time with Him, or do you listen to your own desire to stay in bed and push the snooze button over and over again until it's too late to have a quiet time?

Loving our King is first an act of the will, a choice to put Him first, no matter what our feelings may say.

> *I delight to do Your will, O my God…*
> **PSALM 40:8**

2. Be Willing to Make Sacrifices

> The best time for most people is early morning – not because most of us love jumping out of bed, but because it is the only time of day when we can be fairly sure of not being interrupted and because it is best to commune with God before you commune with people. Your attitude toward them will then arise out of your life in Him. Offering to God the first hour of the day is a token of consecration of all of our time.[3]
>
> **Elisabeth Elliot**

Scripture puts a high value on waking up early, even before dawn, and giving the first fruits of our day to God in prayer, worship, and seeking His face:

O God, You are my God; early will I seek You;
my soul thirsts for You…
PSALM 63:1

Awake, my glory! Awake, lute and harp!
I will awaken the dawn.
PSALM 57:8

[The virtuous woman] also rises while it is yet night…
PROVERBS 31:15

Jesus Himself set for us a clear example of rising early to seek the Father's face: "Now in the morning, having risen a long while before daylight, He went out and departed to a solitary place; and there He prayed" (Mk. 1:35).

There is something so right about rising early to seek God in prayer. It is the ultimate way to *deny self*; to silence our excuses and yield to the Spirit of God. (See Matthew 16:24.) It's an opportunity to declare with our lives, not just our lips, that Jesus truly is our most important priority – it gives the Spirit of God the first say over our time and priorities.

If it is truly not possible for you to build prayer into your early mornings, then designate another time during the day when you can be relatively sure you won't be interrupted. The keys to a disciplined prayer life are regularity, consistency, and commitment!

John "Praying" Hyde said, "Early in the morning, at four or five o-clock, and late at night to twelve or one o'clock – in college or at parties at home, I used to keep such hours for myself or pleasure – can I not do as much for God and souls?"[4] What convicting words! Are we willing to make daily personal sacrifices in order to put our relationship with Christ first?

3. Gather the Right Tools

Spend some time thinking through what tools could assist you in having more effective prayer and quiet times. Can you set aside an area of the house that is quiet and free from distractions? Can you download some worship music or audio Scripture to listen to while you pray and meditate upon Him? (*The Word of Promise* is one of my favorite audio Bibles because it is professionally dramatized and enhanced with beautiful music.) Starting out a prayer time by playing a few of the Psalms from an audio Bible has proven a wonderful tool to help usher me into the presence of God. It can also be helpful to grow your understanding in learning how to handle basic Bible study tools. A great place to start is by familiarizing yourself with BlueLetterBible.org, as there are many resources designed to help you unlock the meanings of the original languages.

I love to keep a prayer journal because it allows me to record the faithfulness of God in my life. Whenever I am walking through a season where my faith is being tested, it is uplifting to read back over my journal throughout the past years or months, and see how many times God has come through for me.

Ask God to show you the practical things you can do to not only guard your daily appointment with Him, but also to make that time as powerful and Christ-centered as possible.

4. Embrace Godly Discipline

> *But I discipline my body and bring it into subjection, lest, when I have preached to others, I myself should become disqualified.*
> **1 CORINTHIANS 9:27**

The word *discipline* has almost become taboo in today's modern Christian world. It conjures up images of legalism and lists of rules and regulations. Yet godly discipline is nothing of the sort. It is an act of worship – crucifying our selfish agenda in order to surrender to Christ's pure and perfect agenda. (See Romans 12:1.) Discipline does not bring misery and restriction into our life. Rather, it brings glorious freedom. When our bodies and emotions are subject to the Spirit of

God, we are free to live as He calls us to live rather than being enslaved to our selfish desires. We are able to give our time, our energy, and our lives fully to the things of His Kingdom.

During the seasons of my life in which I have embraced a disciplined lifestyle as an act of worship, my intimacy with Christ has flourished. But whenever I say, "It doesn't matter how much time I spend in prayer," I find that my relationship with Him slips to the back burner, and I end up talking a lot *about* Him without really *knowing* Him. It is not the mere act of "being disciplined" that draws me close to Christ. But discipline allows me to hear His voice, understand His truth, and connect with His heart in a way that is impossible when I'm controlled by selfishness and apathy.

It is important to recognize that godly discipline and human willpower are two different things. Human willpower only lasts temporarily and is dependent upon our own ability. Godly discipline goes far beyond mere human "oomph" and comes through yielding to His Spirit and relying on His grace. It is impossible in our own strength. There have been many early mornings when I have whispered, "Lord, I do not have the energy to get out of bed. Please infuse me with Your strength. Give me the grace to do what You have called me to do!" Whenever I pray this prayer, I find that He enables me by His grace to do what would otherwise be impossible in my own strength.

Even if personal discipline doesn't come naturally for you, remember that anyone can embrace godly discipline. All you must do is take steps of obedience and call upon Him for the strength and grace to do what you could never do on your own.

Seven Practicals to Start Building a Lifestyle of Godly Discipline

1. Meditate on Truth

It can be helpful to memorize a simple Scripture and train yourself to recite it the moment your alarm goes off in the morning. If you're looking for a place to start, Psalm 118:24 is a great one!

2. Recruit an Accountability Partner

Pray for God to show you or bring someone into your life with whom you can honestly share areas in your life that need greater discipline and who will be able to provide you with accountability to help you grow in these areas. Having a trusted friend with whom you can share your failures and successes can make a tremendous difference in helping you cultivate a more disciplined lifestyle, enabled by God's grace.

3. Start Gradually

A wisdom tip for implementing greater discipline into your daily lifestyle is to not make drastic changes overnight! If you are convicted to make practical changes in your life that will enable you to seek Jesus more fully, break those goals down into small, achievable steps and begin applying them into your life, by His grace.

For example, if you are used to waking up at nine o'clock and try to switch to a five o'clock alarm, chances are you will wane in your commitment after a day or two. Instead, try setting your alarm for 20 minutes earlier for the first couple of days. Then, set it for another 20 minutes earlier and work on that new discipline for a few days.

4. Guarding the Secret Place

But you, when you pray, go into your room, and when you have shut your door, pray to your Father who is in the secret place; and your Father who sees in secret will reward you openly.
MATTHEW 6:6

Scripture has much to say about keeping secrets. Giving in secret, praying in secret, meeting God in the secret place, and guarding secrets that are entrusted to us. Here are just a few additional examples:

… do not appear to men to be fasting, but to your Father who is in the secret place; and your Father who sees in secret will reward you openly.
MATTHEW 6:18

A gift in secret pacifies anger...
PROVERBS 21:14

He who dwells in the secret place of the Most High
shall abide under the shadow of the Almighty.
PSALM 91:1

Even Jesus kept secrets, as well as charged others to do so. On various occasions He commanded His disciples not to tell others that He was the Christ, after they had seen amazing signs that convinced them. (See Matthew 16:20; Mark 8:30; Mark 9:9.) And when He healed various people, He told them not to tell anyone what had happened. (See Luke 5:14 and 8:56.)

And yet, despite these Scriptural exhortations toward secret-keeping, being guarded is not en vogue these days, even in Christian circles. It is often seen as far more healthy and right to share everything, to be open about everything, and never keep anything to yourself. Just as a marriage relationship cannot thrive if a couple does not guard the privacy of their relationship, our relationship with Christ cannot thrive if we do not keep sacred things sacred in our walk with Him.

Amy Carmichael, speaking of a private personal struggle: "I am dispirited. I cannot speak to anyone of the cause. It is private." And God's answer was, "I heard thee in the secret place of the storm. In the secret place among the unspoken things, there I am."[5]

Of course there may be times when He leads you to share some of your personal journey with other people. But let Him first prove Himself as the All-Sufficient One in your life. Learn how to make Him your first turn and your true Comforter before you rush to process or share with other people.

Mary, the mother of Jesus, was a beautiful example of abiding "in the secret place." From the moment the angel first came to her, there wasn't anyone else in her life who could truly relate to what she was going through. When she was found to be with child, most people in her life probably assumed it was a result of her sinful choice, rather than a miracle of God. Yet she did not rush to defend herself or explain her situation to others. She remained yielded and obedient to God's will, even when her circumstances became very difficult.

Later, when she had seen and experienced many incredible things, she chose to keep them quiet rather than publish them to the world. "But Mary kept all these things and pondered them in her heart," it says Luke 2:19. I've often wondered if one of the reasons Mary was chosen to be the mother of Jesus was because of this rare quality of discretion and guardedness. She knew how to keep sacred things sacred. I believe we can learn so much from her amazing example of secret-keeping.

Suggesting that they take time to prayerfully consider what they share, when they share, and why they share can help those in your group identify if they are going too "public" with what Jesus is teaching them in the secret place.

5. Don't Let Failure Deter You

Most of us will go through unusual seasons in which regular, consistent prayer just doesn't happen. It may be the birth of a child, a difficult pregnancy, a hospital stay, a family emergency, and so on, when every spare moment of our time and energy is given to "survival mode."

When life seems to buck me off my normal prayer routine, I have learned to rise up on the strength of God and get back in the saddle as soon as I possibly can. Instead of feeling like I somehow have to play "spiritual catch up" when I haven't spent much time in prayer for a while, I rest in the comforting fact that I can pick up right where I left off. No matter what I have walked through, my God is unchanging and He is always ready and waiting for me to cast my cares upon Him!

6. Choose the Important Over the Urgent

On two different occasions, the disciples fished all night long and caught nothing. But when Jesus came and stood in their midst, they let down their net once and caught such an abundance that they didn't even have room in their boat to contain it all. (See Luke 5:4-7 and John 21:3-6.)

When prayer is missing from our life and we are controlled by the tyranny of the urgent, we spend countless time and energy trying to make our life work, constantly failing, and beating our head against the wall in frustration. But as it says in Psalm 1, when we meditate upon our Lord day and night, we become like a tree that *"brings forth its fruit"* (v.3) – and everything that we do just somehow works. Life becomes fruitful instead of frustrating.

Next time you are tempted to choose busyness over prayer, remember the secret to making life work: *putting Jesus first.*

7. Tune Out the Enemy's Voice

> *For the weapons of our warfare are not carnal but mighty in God for pulling down strongholds, casting down arguments and every high thing that exalts itself against the knowledge of God, bringing every thought into captivity to the obedience of Christ…*
> **2 CORINTHIANS 10:4-5**

The book of Nehemiah provides an amazing picture of resisting the enemy's lies. As Nehemiah was rebuilding the wall around Jerusalem, his enemies mocked him, distracted him, and threatened him. They sent false prophets to warn him that he must flee into the temple to hide. They accused him of rebelling against the king. They attempted to scare him by saying an army was coming to slay him in the night. Yet each time, Nehemiah met their lies with truth and continued in what God had called him to do. As a result, his enemies' plots came to nothing and Nehemiah succeeded in the work that God had called him to do.

Don't be surprised if the enemy attacks you when you take steps forward to pursue Jesus Christ. Leonard Ravenhill said, "Men of prayer must be men of steel, for they will be assaulted by Satan even before they attempt to assault his kingdom."[5] This principle also applies to us as women!

Be on guard and ready to fight Satan's lies with God's truth. As you make a habit of tuning out the enemy's "noise" and doing what you know God has called you to do, you will be successful in your spiritual pursuits, just as Nehemiah was successful in building the wall.

THIS WEEK

Read Luke 10:38-42:
Now it happened as they went that He entered a certain village; and a certain woman named Martha welcomed Him into her house. And she had a sister called Mary, who also sat at Jesus' feet and heard His word. But Martha was distracted with much serving, and she approached Him and said, 'Lord, do You not care that my sister has left me to serve alone? Therefore tell her to help me.' And Jesus answered and said to her, 'Martha, Martha, you are worried and troubled about many things. But one thing is needed, and Mary has chosen that good part, which will not be taken away from her.'

Reflect: Am I taking time each day to sit at Jesus' feet? Am I allowing distractions to pull me away from intimacy with Him? What practical steps can I take to make Him my highest priority?

Read Matthew 6:6:
'But you, when you pray, go into your room, and when you have shut your door, pray to your Father who is in the secret place; and your Father who sees in secret will reward you openly.'

Reflect: Do I know how to meet God alone in the secret place, or am I in the habit of always turning to people to process my struggles? Are there any practical steps I need to take in order to preserve the sacred intimacy in my relationship with Him?

Soul-Searching Questions
Am I too busy to pray, or too busy NOT to pray?

What changes should I make to my daily life in order to "have an appointment with the Lord and keep it"?

WEEK 4: INTIMACY

_____
_____
_____

Are there things I need to say *no* to in order to say *yes* to time in God's presence?

_____
_____
_____
_____

What are the biggest distractions in my life that hinder me from spending time with Him?

_____
_____
_____
_____

Have I been led by emotion or godly discipline when it comes to my prayer life?

_____
_____
_____
_____

Am I ready to let God's grace enable me to embrace spiritual discipline instead of rejecting it? How will this change my relationship with Him?

_____
_____
_____
_____

Take it Deeper

The following resources have been selected to enhance your journey through this lesson and take these truths deeper into your heart.

Read *Tramp for the Lord* by Corrie ten Boom.
Q. What stands out to you about her personal, daily walk with Christ? What enabled her to be so in tune with God's voice? What can you learn from her example when it comes to intimacy with Christ?

Watch or listen to *The 9 Lies* by Eric Ludy available for free download at Ellerslie.com to learn more about tuning out the enemy's voice.

Read the *Sweeter Than Honey* Bible study article series available at SetApartGirl.com. This guided Bible study provides practicals for how to build your daily quiet times, while casting a beautiful vision for the importance of studying God's Word, that truly is sweeter than honey!

Other books to take the message deeper:

Wrestling Prayer: A Passionate Communion with God by Eric and Leslie Ludy

Discipline: The Glad Surrender by Elisabeth Elliot

E. M. Bounds Complete Works on Prayer by E. M. Bounds

The Tyranny of the Urgent by Charles Hummel

Week Five

Devotion – Fixing Your Gaze Completely on Jesus

See that you walk circumspectly, not as fools but as wise, redeeming the time, because the days are evil.
EPHESIANS 5:15-16

[The virtuous woman] … does not eat the bread of idleness.
PROVERBS 31:27

Only one life; twill soon be passed. Only what's done for Christ will last.[1]

C. T. Studd

It is easy to find out whether our lives are focused, and if so, where the focus lies. Where do our thoughts settle when consciousness comes back in the morning? Where do they swing back when the pressure is off during the day? Dare to have it out with God, and ask Him to show you whether or not all is focused on Christ and His glory. Turn your soul's vision to Jesus, and look and look at Him, and a strange dimness will come over all that is apart from Him.[2]

Lilias Trotter

How Can You Tell Where Your True Focus Lies?

The things of earth (i.e. popularity, comforts, frivolity, success) will grow strangely dim when your eyes are truly fixed upon Him.

…in Your presence is fullness of joy; at Your right hand are pleasures forevermore.
PSALM 16:11

As modern Christians, it often seems perfectly normal for us to build our lives around worldly entertainment, letting movies, TV, music, magazines, novels, social media, and professional sports consume the vast majority of our free time. But when we become entangled with the inordinate affections of our culture, it is impossible for us to seek Jesus Christ with an undivided heart. God makes it clear that we cannot love both Him *and* the things of this world:

> *Adulterers and adulteresses! Do you not know that friendship with the world is enmity with God? Whoever therefore wants to be a friend of the world makes himself an enemy of God.*
> JAMES 4:4

> *Do not love the world or the things in the world. If anyone loves the world, the love of the Father is not in him. For all that is in the world – the lust of the flesh, the lust of the eyes, and the pride of life – is not of the Father but is of the world.*
> 1 JOHN 2:15-16

It might seem that living a life that is not built around worldly entertainment would be dull, or that not watching TV regularly and failing to follow everything that happens on social media would cause you to become out of touch with the culture and unable to impact the world for Christ. But I have discovered that the opposite is true. Once I let go of my addiction to pop-culture entertainment, I suddenly had time to pursue Christ with all my heart; I became free to live the exciting adventure He had planned for me each day. And once I stopped assaulting my spiritual senses with the ungodly messages of the culture, I became much more in tune with the voice of God's Spirit and far more equipped to make a lasting impact on the world around me.

If you desire an undivided heart toward Christ and deeper intimacy with Him, I encourage you to prayerfully consider any areas of pop-culture that have become unhealthy addictions in your life such as music, movies, social media, TV shows, sports, novels, and so on. Ask God to show you what activities need to be removed from your life, and what activities might need to be put in their proper place.

Key Questions to Ask About Leisure Activities

1. Is this activity distracting me from Christ or causing me to adopt the ungodly values of the world? If my answer is *yes*, then I shouldn't be doing it!
2. Am I turning to this activity for fulfillment instead of to Christ? If my answer is *yes*, then I need to reevaluate where I'm looking for satisfaction. There may not be anything particularly wrong with an activity, but if it's replacing your relationship with Christ, your priorities are off balance.

Stewarding the Gift of Time

God has entrusted us with the precious gift of time. Twenty-four hours in every day; seven days in every week; each day significant, each hour important, and each moment of value to God. How many of those moments are being spent on things that matter in light of eternity? Only when we are willing to give God the best hours of our day — rather than whatever is left after we have wasted most of our time on earthly things — will we experience vibrant intimacy with our Heavenly King and become the set apart women He has called us to be.

1. Identify Time Wasters

Many of us look at our daily schedules and can't see any available time for seeking God or sharing the Gospel with others. But so often, our lives are filled with distractions and time wasters that take up far more of our free time than we realize. Social media, Internet surfing, phone chats, movies, and TV are a few of the most common culprits. Again, it's not that these mediums are always wrong in themselves, but if not put in their proper place, they can dominate our time and pull us away from building our lives around God's priorities. When we aren't guarded in these areas, we often waste our time on temporal things, without even realizing we are doing so.

If you find yourself wondering where all your time has gone, consider keeping a diary of your daily activities, especially the things you spend your free time on. For a week or two, write down exactly how much time you spend on the phone, emailing, texting, on Facebook, on Pinterest, posting on Instagram, watching movies, channel surfing, reading magazines, and so on. Don't just guess at how much time you are spending on these things. Set a timer or monitor the clock as you do them, and write down the exact number of minutes or hours being spent on each activity. Then, prayerfully evaluate whether you need to cut or reduce any of these potential time wasters from your daily life.

For we are His workmanship, created in Christ Jesus for good works, which God prepared beforehand that we should walk in them.
EPHESIANS 2:10

But she who lives in pleasure is dead while she lives.
1 TIMOTHY 5:6

2. Refuel the Right Way

As busy women, we often find ourselves in need of rest, perspective, and new strength. It's tempting to try to do things that have no eternal value, yet will distract us temporarily.

Always remember, when we take time alone to refresh and refuel, it should flow from a motive of becoming even stronger and more equipped to serve Jesus Christ, not simply to escape from the responsibilities of serving and godly living. Certainly there is nothing wrong with doing practical things in order to refuel and recharge. A long walk, a refreshing bike ride, an hour journaling outside in God's creation, an encouraging chat with a trusted friend, or a family vacation can be wonderful ways to gain clearer perspective. But it's important not to give into the voice that whispers, "You deserve some self-indulgence right now. Forget about everyone else. Put your spiritual life on hold for a while. Take time for YOU!"

I have learned that the best "me time" is not actually "me time" at all, but rather "God time." Spending time in His presence – journaling, worshiping, studying Scripture – produces far more lasting refreshment to my soul than an hour on social media or vegging in front of a movie ever could. Remember, there should be no area of our lives that we claim as "ours" – even our leisure time! Every area of our lives should belong to God. When we say *no* to frivolous activities in order to say *yes* to time in God's presence, we will find the strength, joy, and peace we need for the daily battles we are called to fight. Next time you feel in need of some "me time", stop and consider what will truly refresh you at the soul level. Practice going to the feet of Jesus instead of to the comforts of this world, and you will discover that in His presence really is the fullness of joy!

As you go about your daily life, prayerfully examine the motives behind *why* you spend time doing the things that you do. When evaluating any activity, ask yourself these questions: *Am I doing this for selfish reasons, or Christ-honoring ones? Is this activity frivolous, or does it serve a higher purpose?*

Here are some ways you can tell whether something has eternal value:
- It causes you to draw closer to Jesus Christ and/or learn more about Him.
- It builds meaningful relationships with people God has put in your life.
- It helps you bless others and assists you in sharing the love of Christ with them.
- It helps you become better equipped for the things God has called you to.
- It leaves you peacefully refreshed instead of agitated and distracted.
- It bears "good fruit" instead of "bad fruit" in your life. (See Galatians 5:19-26.)

> *Turn away my eyes from looking at worthless things,*
> *and revive me in Your way.*
> **PSALM 119:37**

We often ask the question "what is the harm of it" when it comes to certain pastimes, to taking our recreation in certain ways. What is the harm of the latest novel, even if it happens to be rather unprofitable? And we who have not the time to read one out of a thousand of the real books that have been written, spend a precious hour by deliberate choice on things not worthwhile. The question "what is the harm of it" falls from us and is forgotten when we look at Him, the risen-again Raboni of our souls![3]

AMY CARMICHAEL

The Bible says that even the small areas of our lives, like eating and drinking, should be done for His glory and not our own selfish pleasure. (See 1 Corinthians 10:31.) When you allow your daily activities to serve God's purposes for your life rather than your own, you will begin to gain an eternal focus in everything you do.

WEEK 5: DEVOTION

THIS WEEK

Read Mark 1:35:
Now in the morning, having risen a long while before daylight, He went out and departed to a solitary place; and there He prayed.

Read Mark 6:46:
And when He had sent them away, He departed to the mountain to pray.

Reflect: What can I learn from Jesus' example of refueling? Am I running to the distractions of the world or to the feet of Jesus for true rest? What can I do to change any wrong patterns in this area?

Read Psalm 119:37:
Turn away my eyes from looking at worthless things, and revive me in Your way.

Reflect: Have I been looking at the worthless things of this culture instead of at Jesus? In what ways? How can I redirect the gaze of my soul?

Read Acts 7:54-56:
When they heard these things they were cut to the heart, and they gnashed at him with their teeth. But he, being full of the Holy Spirit, gazed into heaven and saw the glory of God, and Jesus standing at the right hand of God, and said, "Look! I see the heavens opened and the Son of Man standing at the right hand of God!"

Reflect: What can I learn from Stephen's example of fixing his gaze on Jesus, even in the midst of mockery and hatred from others?

Soul-Searching Questions

Am I addicted to pop-culture entertainment and distractions (Netflix, movies, TV, video games, social media, YouTube, etc.)? If so, what might God be asking me to do in order to come away from these addictions?

In what areas of my life do I need to exchange a temporal focus for an eternal focus? (Reference the list on page 53 for guidance.)

Have I been settling for counterfeit peace and joy? Am I willing to find my joy, peace, satisfaction, and rest in Christ instead of trivial distractions? What changes do I feel He is asking me to make in order to do this?

Take it Deeper

The following resources have been selected to enhance your journey through this lesson and take these truths deeper into your heart.

Read *God's Missionary* by Amy Carmichael.
Q. How does coming away from the world in areas like recreation and entertainment strengthen my relationship with Christ and my ability to reach others for Him?

Listen to the episode *Learning to Rest the Right Way* on the Set Apart Girl Podcast (available at SetApartGirl.com) for more inspiration on how to leverage your free-time activities for true refreshment in Him.

Watch or listen to *A Friday Night in the Promised Land* a free sermon by Eric Ludy available at Ellerslie.com.
Q. Are you willing use *all your time* for God's glory instead of personal pleasure?

Week Six

Radiance – Overcoming Insecurity Through the Crucified Life

*...the incorruptible beauty of a gentle and quiet spirit,
which is very precious in the sight of God.*
1 PETER 3:4

"Inner Beauty" vs. "Incorruptible Beauty"

Inner Beauty (the culture's definition)

Being confident in who you are; having a positive "sense of self"; appreciating your own uniqueness and personal qualities.

> If a soul has any beauty, it is because Christ has endowed that soul with His own, for in ourselves we are deformed and defiled! There is no beauty in any of us but what our Lord has worked in us.[1]
>
> Charles Spurgeon

There is an entirely different kind of beauty we are called to showcase ... *His*.

Incorruptible Beauty

(literal definition) Uncorrupted (pure) and immortal (of Heaven, not earth).

In other words: Reflecting the purity and nature of Jesus Christ in and through your character and conduct.

To reflect incorruptible beauty in our own strength is impossible. We must be fully yielded and surrendered to Jesus Christ so that HIS radiance and life can be seen through us.

Key Truth

Christianity is not about esteeming self; but denying self and esteeming Christ.

> *'He who finds his life will lose it, and he*
> *who loses his life for My sake will find it.'*
> MATTHEW 10:39

Finds His Life: to find *SELF* by thought, examination, scrutiny, observation, practice, and experience; to see, learn, discover, and understand

This is very similar to the ideas of "self-discovery" and "being true to ourselves" that are so popular today.

Loses His Life: to destroy *SELF*, to put out of the way entirely, to abolish, to render useless

> *…If anyone desires to come after me, let him deny himself…*
> LUKE 9:23

Deny: to forget one's self; lose sight of one's own interests

The Surprising Secret to Overcoming Insecurity

Getting out of the way so that Jesus can be seen through your life. The world says that self-esteem is the answer for our insecurity. But we will only gain lasting security when we look away from ourselves and toward Jesus Christ. The question "Who am I?" is not nearly as important as the question, "Who is He?"

> What I'm called to be is nothing; Jesus made Himself nothing.[2]
> Elisabeth Elliot

> *I am only the friend of the bridegroom; not the bridegroom Himself; when the bridegroom is seen, my joy is complete. He must increase, but I must decrease.*
> JOHN 3:29-30 PARAPHRASE

The opposite of incorruptible beauty — *showcasing self*.

> *A foolish woman is clamorous...*
> PROVERBS 9:13

Clamorous: to make noise, to draw attention to oneself, to cause a stir

To exude the incorruptible beauty of a quiet spirit means to no longer draw attention to yourself, but to keep "self" quiet, so that Jesus can be seen and heard through your life.

> The world looks for happiness through self-assertion. The Christian knows that joy is found in self-abandonment. If a man will let himself be lost for My sake, Jesus said, he will find his true self.[3]
>
> Elisabeth Elliot

> Unless you are prepared to let go of what you are, you'll never become what God intended you to be.[4]
>
> Major Ian Thomas

God desires that we would learn to esteem Jesus Christ, not ourselves. When He is in His rightful place in our lives and hearts, insecurity is replaced with a confidence that cannot be shaken, because it's in Him.

Exchanging Self-Promotion for Christ-Promotion

When we try to be seen and applauded, Jesus fades into the background, and people look at *us*, not Him. But when we focus on getting out of the way and pointing others to Him, He receives the glory He deserves.

What About Talents?

This doesn't mean we can never cultivate the unique talents and strengths that He has given us. It is certainly possible to use our gifts to glorify God. (In fact, that is why He gave them to us in the first place!) But first, we must ask some critical questions: *Am I doing this for His glory or for my own applause? When people see this part of my life, are they drawn closer to Jesus, or are they merely impressed with me?*

God doesn't measure success the way we do. Mary of Bethany poured out her most priceless possession upon the feet of Jesus without applause, recognition, or fanfare, and some thought it was a waste. Yet Jesus said, in essence, "What she has done for me is a picture of the Gospel itself." (See Mark 14:3-9.) The Apostle Paul had loads of accomplishments and accolades that he could have leveraged to gain a bigger platform for his ministry. But only when he was willing to consider his earthly achievements worthless and become a "fool for Christ's sake" was he truly effective as a witness of the Gospel. (See 1 Corinthians 1:26-28.) Jesus said that if we cling to our lives, we will lose them, but if we are willing to give up our lives for His sake, we will find true life. (See Matthew 10:39.)

Instead of striving to be noticed and appreciated, we are to take an entirely different posture into every area of our life, one of humility and self-denial. Whether we are recognized and applauded, or disregarded and overlooked, it should make no difference to us. A woman who has taken up her cross to follow Christ only cares about knowing Him and making Him known.

> If my thoughts revolve around myself … then I know nothing of Calvary love. If I cannot in honest happiness take the second place (or twentieth) … then I know nothing of Calvary love.[5]
>
> Amy Carmichael

Taking the Lowest Place

Many of us have been conditioned to believe that self-promotion is right and good, but as set apart women, God has called us to forget ourselves and let all our own interests become swallowed up in Him. We are not to seek the highest place, but the lowest one.

Nowhere in Scripture is this better illustrated than when Jesus humbly took the position of a lowly servant to wash His disciples' feet.

> *Jesus, knowing that the Father had given all things into His hands, and that He had come from God and was going to God, rose from supper and laid aside His garments, took a towel and girded Himself. After that, He poured water into a basin and began to wash the disciples' feet, and to wipe them with the towel with which He was girded.*
> JOHN 13:3-5

"He took a towel," wrote Amy Carmichael, "the Lord of glory did that. Is it the bondservant's business to say which work is large and which is small, which is unimportant and which is worth doing?"[6] Jesus knew exactly who He was – the King over Heaven and earth, with all things under His feet. Yet He willingly humbled Himself and took the lowest position, one of a servant who washed the dirt and mire from the disciples' feet.

Following this astonishing act, He said, "If I then, your Lord and Teacher, have washed your feet, you also ought to wash one another's feet. For I have given you an example, that you should do as I have done to you" (Jn. 13:14-15). Jesus' life was a picture of this kind of humility, of willingly choosing the lowest place rather than the highest one. And He lived this out as an example for us, that we should follow in His steps. (See 1 Peter 2:21.)

Paul reminds us, "Let nothing be done through selfish ambition or conceit, but in lowliness of mind let each esteem others better than himself … let this mind be in you which was also in Christ Jesus, who, being in the form of God … made Himself of no reputation, taking the form of a bondservant and coming in the likeness of men … He humbled Himself and became obedient to the point of death, even the death of the cross" (Phil. 2:3-8).

Imagine the freedom of being unconcerned whether or not people appreciated your unique talents, personality, or acts of service. Imagine if your only concern was making Jesus known, even if no one ever remembered your name.

Again, we will only gain lasting security when we look *away* from ourselves and *toward* Jesus Christ. The question, "Who am *I*?" is not nearly as important as the question, "Who is *He*?"

Scripture is filled with exhortations to exchange self-promotion for humility. Here are just a few samplings:

> *Love ... does not seek its own...*
> **1 CORINTHIANS 13:4-5**

> *For whoever exalts himself will be humbled,*
> *and he who humbles himself will be exalted.*
> **LUKE 14:11**

> *...God opposes the proud, but gives grace to the humble.*
> **JAMES 4:6 ESV**

> *...in lowliness of mind let each esteem others better than himself.*
> **PHILIPPIANS 2:3**

> *...Do not think of yourself more highly than you ought, but rather think of yourself with sober judgment...*
> **ROMANS 12:3 NIV**

> *Let no one seek his own, but each one the other's well-being.*
> **1 CORINTHIANS 10:24**

And yet, there is perhaps nothing more challenging to our flesh (that selfish, sinful part of us that craves control) than to lay down our pride and willingly *"take the lowest place"* as Jesus did. When we choose humility, we are choosing the very attitude of Christ, as it says in

Philippians 2:5. And there is no better way for the beauty of Heaven to come cascading through our lives than to get out of the way so that He can be clearly seen.

THIS WEEK

Read Philippians 2:5-7:
Let this mind be in you which was also in Christ Jesus, who, being in the form of God, did not consider it robbery to be equal with God, but made Himself of no reputation, taking the form of a bondservant, and coming in the likeness of men. And being found in appearance as a man, He humbled Himself...

Reflect: Have I been preserving my reputation, or laying it down as Jesus did? Am I willing to follow in Christ's footsteps of self-denial and humility?

Read James 4:6:
...'God resists the proud, but gives grace to the humble.'

Reflect: In what ways can I choose the path of humility instead of self-promotion? How will this promote lasting confidence in my life?

Read Philippians 2:3:
Let nothing be done through selfish ambition or conceit, but in lowliness of mind let each esteem others better than himself.

Reflect: Does God need to cleanse any selfish ambition or conceit from my life? In what areas?

Soul-Searching Questions
Am I willing to decrease that He might increase in my life? What does that mean for me practically?

_____

_____

_____

WEEK 6: RADIANCE

In what ways do I need to get out of the way so that He can be clearly seen through my life?

Have I been seeking to showcase my own beauty and goodness to others? How can I allow His beauty to shine through me instead?

How will cultivating Christ-centered beauty help me overcome insecurity?

Take it Deeper

The following resources have been selected to enhance your journey through this lesson and take these truths deeper into your heart.

Watch the sermon *Feminine Beauty* by Eric Ludy available at Ellerslie.com.
Q. Am I building my femininity after God's pattern? In what ways must I allow Him to reshape this area of my life?

Listen to *Let Me Be a Woman* or *A Woman's Gifts* – messages by Elisabeth Elliot on biblical womanhood at BlueLetterBible.org.
Q. How does the Christ-centered femininity Elisabeth talks about challenge or change your view of femininity as God intended?

Other books to take the message deeper:
Set Apart Femininity by Leslie Ludy
The Set Apart Woman by Leslie Ludy
The Lost Art of True Beauty by Leslie Ludy
Let Me Be a Woman by Elisabeth Elliot

Week Seven

Discretion – Adopting a Christ-Honoring Pattern for Digital Conduct

...admonish the young women to ... be discreet...
TITUS 2:4-5

*But I say to you that for every idle word men may speak,
they will give account of it in the day of judgment.*
MATTHEW 12:36

Adopting a Digital Code of Conduct

Even though there are no specific guidelines in Scripture about how to handle the area of social media, there are many biblical principles that give us a clear picture of how we can honor our King in our digital lives. It is key to adopt a "digital code of conduct" – a predetermined list of principles that help to govern your decisions and actions on social media. When you encounter new and trendy digital fads, these principles can help protect you from being swept away by the culture's relentless pressure to let down your guard in this ever-present area of life.

Principle #1: Choose Your Words Wisely

Proverbs 29:20 gives us a serious warning about being careless and unguarded with our words: "Do you see a man hasty in his words? There is more hope for a fool than for him." And Jesus reminds us of this principle again in Matthew 12:36: "...every idle word that men shall speak, they shall give account thereof in the day of judgment." Those are sobering verses to consider in light of how thoughtlessly we often treat our tweets, texts, and posts! If we want to honor God in our digital communication, the first step is to learn how to weigh our words in light of eternity.

In 1 Timothy 5:13, Paul warns against the ungodly behavior of certain women in the church: "…they learn to be idle, wandering about from house to house, and not only idle but also gossips and busybodies, saying things which they ought not." Now let's imagine this verse with a slightly modern twist: "…they learn to be idle, wandering about from **Facebook page to Facebook page**, being gossips and busybodies, **posting things** which they ought not."

In 2 Timothy 2:16, Paul commands, "…shun profane and idle babblings, for they will increase to more ungodliness." The term "idle babbling" here means *empty discussion, discussion of vain and useless matters.* What a perfect description of much of our online communication! Bantering about frivolous topics and posting about pop-culture trivia may seem harmless, but we must remember that one day we must give an account for every single idle word we speak *and* post.

So what kind of words *should* we be posting on social media?

In Romans 14:19 Paul exhorts us, "Therefore, let us pursue the things which make for peace and the things by which one may edify another." The word "edify" here means *to build someone up in their faith, to promote another person's growth in Christian wisdom, piety, holiness, and so on.* And in Ephesians 4:29 he tells us, "Let no corrupt word proceed out of your mouth, but what is good for necessary edification, that it may impart grace to the hearers."

We can only glorify God with our words when we use them to edify other people rather than to simply fill space, make ourselves heard, or engage in gossip and worldly banter. Proverbs 25:11 says, "A word fitly spoken is like apples of gold in settings of silver." Just as the wrong words can pull both us and our onlookers away from God, the right words can draw us closer to Him.

A great way to evaluate whether your texts, tweets, and posts are truly edifying and "fitting" is to hold them up against Paul's checklist in Philippians 4:8: "…whatever things are true, whatever things are noble, whatever things are just, whatever things are pure, whatever things are lovely, whatever things are of good report, if there is any virtue and if there is anything praiseworthy – meditate on these things."

Principle #2: Choose Discretion

While authenticity is important among Christians, there is nothing God-honoring about publicly venting our frustrations to the world. In fact, the Bible says the opposite: "A fool vents all his feelings, but a wise man holds them back" (Prov. 29:11).

Clearly, there is a right way and a wrong way to be "authentic and real" with our Christian brothers and sisters. Privately sharing our struggles with a trusted godly mentor, spiritual authority, or prayer partner can be healthy and good. But publicly venting them, without any guardedness or discretion, is not.

Proverbs 11:22 paints a jarring picture of a woman who shares everything with everyone: "As a ring of gold in a swine's snout, so is a lovely woman who lacks discretion." In contrast, Mary the mother of Jesus shows us a refreshing picture of feminine guardedness: "But Mary kept all these things and pondered them in her heart" (Lk. 2:19). If anyone had a reason to rush around the countryside and spill her guts to all her friends, it was Mary. She'd seen and experienced many amazing and noteworthy things. But she chose to guard the sacred things in her life, rather than openly broadcast them. Perhaps her discretion was one of the reasons she found favor with God and was chosen for such a task as bringing up the Savior of the world!

The bottom line is this: if you are looking for a place to "pour out your heart," don't turn to social media or blogging as your outlet. Your first turn should be to God, as it says in Psalm 62:8: "…pour out your heart before Him; God is a refuge for us." And then, if additional support is needed, find trusted godly people you can meet with privately to process through your struggles. Venting your emotions online is like turning your diary inside out for the world to see. Remember that it is not just "authenticity" that God praises, but also discretion. The two cannot be separated – especially in our digital communication.

Principle #3: Showcase Christ, Not Self

In light of the biblical call toward humility and self-denial, many of us need to completely shift our approach to social media. If you have been using digital communication to draw attention to yourself, flirt with guys, or become more popular, then you have not been using it in an honorable way. It's not necessarily wrong to share personal stories, life tidbits, or photos of yourself from time to time. But your motive with everything you post or share should be to point the gaze of others toward Christ and not yourself. Ask God to show you how you can "decrease" so that He can "increase" in your digital communication. Even if you are not specifically posting something about the Bible or about Christ, your desire should always be for people to see less of you, and more of Him.

Principle #4: Guard Your Eyes

On social media – or anywhere on the Internet for that matter – we must be extra vigilant about turning our eyes away from the "worthless things" that dominate those platforms: sensuality, crudeness, perversity, worldly enticements, celebrity worship, etc. When we love the world and the things that are in the world, we cannot love God with our whole heart. (See 1 John 2:15.) When we allow worldly things to entice and distract us, we become consumed by "the lust of the flesh, the lust of the eyes, and the pride of life" as it says in 1 John 2:16, and it is impossible to keep our eyes fixed upon Christ with an undivided heart.

If you find certain areas of social media are constantly tempting you to dwell on worthless things and pulling you into worldly distractions, then make a purposeful effort to avoid those pages. And when you do encounter something sensual, crude, or worldly online – don't even take a moment to ponder whether it's worth taking a second look. Practice immediately "turning your eyes away" – whether that means clicking off the page or closing your computer altogether. Remember that the health of your soul and your relationship with Christ are not worth jeopardizing for *anything* – especially things as worthless and temporal as the lust of the flesh and the lust of the eyes.

Principle #5: Put Social Media in its Place

Ephesians 2:10 tells us that we have been created for "good works, which God prepared beforehand that we should walk in them." Sadly, too many of us are missing out on the real-life adventure God has planned for us each day because we are wasting our time in a virtual reality instead. It's high time that we learn to get our phones out of our faces so that we can truly *see* the needs of those God has placed right in front of us!

WEEK 7: DISCRETION

I encourage you to prayerfully consider how much time you should be devoting to social media and to put clear boundaries around your digital life. Recruit an accountability partner if needed, or post reminders on your computer and your desk. Be sure that you are not making more time for online communication than for the most important things in life – like your relationship with Christ and with those He has called you to serve.

When you spend time on social media, set a timer or alarm so that you don't linger longer than you should. And when you are engaged in a more important activity – like prayer, Bible study, or serving others – don't let those dings on your phone or computer distract you! Instead, close your computer, silence your phone, and ask God for the grace to "be all there" as Jim Elliot said.

THIS WEEK

Read 1 Timothy 5:6:
But she who lives in pleasure is dead while she lives.

Reflect: Has social media been causing me to live for temporal pleasure and worldly distractions? In what ways?

Read Ephesians 5:15-16:
See then that you walk circumspectly, not as fools but as wise, redeeming the time, because the days are evil.

Reflect: In what ways has social media been a timewaster in my life? What changes can I make, by God's grace, in order to redeem the time on this earth that He has given me?

Read Luke 2:19:
But Mary kept all these things and pondered them in her heart.

Reflect: Do I keep sacred things sacred, or have I been using social media to publicly share things that should be kept private? What can I learn from Mary's example?

Soul-Searching Questions
Have I been engaging in ungodly patterns on social media? If so, how is God directing me to change this area of my life? What sites do I need to avoid from now on?

_____

_____

_____

_____

_____

WEEK 7: DISCRETION

Do I need accountability for my social media usage? How can I practically invite that accountability into my life?

_____
_____
_____
_____
_____
_____

Have I used social media as a way to draw attention to *self* instead of to Christ? What needs to change in this area?

_____
_____
_____
_____
_____
_____

Has social media become an idol or addiction in my life? Am I willing to lay it down or step away from it (forever or for a season) if God leads me to?

_____
_____
_____
_____
_____
_____

Do I need to limit my time on social media? In what ways?

What specific digital code of conduct is God asking me to adopt?

Take it Deeper

The following resources have been selected to enhance your journey through this lesson and take these truths deeper into your heart.

Read *If* by Amy Carmichael.
Q. If I lived according to the principles in this book, how would my conduct on social media change? Do I believe God can give me the grace to make these changes?

Listen to *Turning Down Digital Noise* – an episode of the Set Apart Girl Podcast available at SetApartGirl.com.
Q. Do my electronic devices interrupt my quiet time with Jesus? What protections do I need to build into my life in order to put Jesus in His rightful place?

Read *Upward and Outward* – an article by Annie Wesche available at SetApartGirl.com.
Q. In what ways is God calling me to turn my gaze upwards towards Him and outwards towards those He has placed in my life?

Other resources to take the message deeper:
Social Media: How to Glorify God in Your Digital Conduct – Online Course with Leslie Ludy

Week Eight
Nobility – Honoring God and Others with Every Word Spoken

Death and life are in the power of the tongue...
PROVERBS 18:21

God has a lot to say about the importance of words. In fact, some of the strongest statements in the Bible have to do with the words we speak. In James, we are told, "…If anyone does not stumble in word, he is a perfect man, able also to bridle the whole body" (Jms. 3:2). As Christians seeking to live set apart, God-honoring lives, we often focus on our outward decisions while overlooking the words that come out of our mouths on a daily basis. Yet this verse reveals that if we do not stumble in our words, we will not stumble in the other areas of our lives. This begs the questions: Are we weighing our words in light of eternity? *Are we treating them with the same importance that God does?*

Perhaps one of the most startling and convicting statements Jesus made was this: "…I say to you that every idle word men may speak, they will give account of it in the day of judgment. For by your words you will be justified, and by your words you will be condemned" (Matt. 12:36-37). How often do we think of the idle, thoughtless words that we casually speak (or post online) as being among the things that will be examined before the God of the universe on Judgment Day?

Speaking God-honoring, life-giving, truth-filled words should not merely be an afterthought in our Christian walk, but an intentional focus by the grace of God. If death and life are in the power of the tongue, then let's choose to use our tongue for life.

Three Key Ways to Speak Life

1. Speak God's Reality

When we speak words that are *not* noble, lovely, or of good report, we cannot meditate on the things God has called us to mediate on. Speaking negative words causes us to focus only on our frustrations and complaints. And predicting negative things that might happen is the equivalent of stating that we don't believe God is going before us or faithfully caring for us as He has promised to.

The words we speak reveal where we are putting our faith. With our words, we either choose to agree with God's promises or accept the enemy's lies. And when we accept the enemy's lies, we give him legal right to harass and hinder our lives. That's why declaring doom and failure over our lives (or the lives of our children) is setting the stage for it to happen. But on the flip side, declaring *God's* reality sets the stage for His power and faithfulness to be experienced.

Speaking God's reality has nothing to do with the "name it, claim it" or "positive affirmation" trends that are often promoted by the culture and even within the church. Those messages usually have selfishness and/or human willpower at the root. (i.e. "If I want something, it's my right to claim it for myself.") Rather, speaking God's reality is a way of honoring our faithful Father by accepting His Word as true. It's looking beyond our circumstances and our fears and declaring that we believe He is exactly who He says He is, and that He cares about the smallest details of our lives. That is when we begin to see miracles unfold in our daily lives – both big and small.

If you have developed a habit of speaking negative things instead of those things that are noble, lovely, and of good report, I encourage you to look for specific promises in God's Word and declare that reality instead.

2. Speak to Edify

Ephesians 4:29 provides God's clear directive for what kinds of conversations we should engage in, "Let no corrupt word proceed out of your mouth, but what is good for necessary edification, that it may impart grace to the hearers."

"Edification" in this verse means to build up another in their faith. In other words, we are to speak things that point others to Christ and not the corrupt patterns of this world. To "impart grace" means to speak things which lead to joy, sweetness, thankfulness, and virtue in the hearers. What a far cry this is from most of our dinner table conversations!

The next time you are in a causal conversation with friends, co-workers, or family members, stop and ask yourself this important question: *Is this conversation truly edifying*? (Hint: If the conversation is dishonoring to others, crude and rude, or pointless and frivolous, the answer to that question is *no*.)

Ideas for Re-Directing Ungodly Conversation:

- Ask the people around you thought-provoking questions, such as: "What has God been teaching you lately?" (if they are believers). Or "Where is the most beautiful place you've traveled?" Showing a genuine interest in others is a wonderful way to edify and build them up, and to reflect the love and attitude of Christ.

- Encourage those around you and tell them things that you appreciate about them. This is especially beneficial in family settings. It's so easy to assume that those closest to us know that we love and appreciate them, but never actually speak those life-giving words to them.

- Don't approach the conversation selfishly. If you are trying to be the center of attention or impress others with your wit and personality, your focus will not be on "imparting grace to your hearers." Instead of pointing others toward Christ you'll be pointing them toward yourself. Remember that even a casual dinner table discussion can be an opportunity to love others as Christ has loved you – with a selfless, sacrificial love. Look for ways to serve others in your conversations, rather than looking for ways others can serve you.

- If all else fails, quietly excuse yourself. There is no reason to participate in a dishonorable conversation because of social obligation. This doesn't mean you need to go away in a huff or storm out of the room in disgust. Be respectful and gracious toward those around you by quietly and discreetly stepping away from a discussion that is not God-honoring.

3. Speak to Honor

> If I can easily discuss the shortcomings and the sins of any other ... if I can in any way slight another in conversation, or even in thought, then I know nothing of Calvary love.[1]
>
> Amy Carmichael

As women, we often fall into the pitfall of dishonoring others with our words under the banner of "just being honest" or showing "loving concern." But the Bible makes it clear that if we are in *any way* slighting another person in conversation, we are not walking in the nature of Christ.

When it comes to something as harmful and destructive as gossip, our answer must always be *no* without any qualifiers or excuses. In other words, the very moment we become aware of the temptation to speak ill of another person, we must call upon the grace of God to say *no* to that bait; to keep our mouth shut, even when the temptation to speak words against someone else is extremely strong. Just because we have strong feelings (i.e. hurt or frustration toward someone) does not mean we need to act upon those feelings. God is ready and willing to enable us with every bit of strength and self-control we need, if we call upon Him.

The same is true for *listening to gossip in any form*. The moment we are aware that someone is attempting to place even the tiniest morsel of gossip in front of us, we must call upon the grace of God to say an immediate and decisive *no* even if it causes social awkwardness. Taking a stand against gossip does *not* mean waiting politely until you've heard all the "dirt" they have to share, and then attempting to sheepishly tell them you don't want to continue the conversation. Rather, it means cutting them off and boldly saying, "I'm sorry but I don't want to hear this, please stop right now" before the person even has a chance to get started. It means literally walking away if they refuse to stop gossiping. And it means withdrawing from friendships that are pulling you into gossip. Yes, this may seem hard to do. But don't forget, gossip and slander are things that God hates. If you truly call upon Him for help in every gossip temptation you face, He is ready to supply you with all the strength you need to follow His pattern.

There are six things the Lord hates, seven that are detestable to Him: haughty eyes, a lying tongue, hands that shed innocent blood, a heart that devises wicked schemes, feet that are quick to rush into evil, a false witness who pours out lies and and a person who stirs up conflict in the community.
PROVERBS 6:16-19 NIV

The one whose walk is blameless, who does what is righteous … whose tongue utters no slander, who does no wrong to a neighbor, and casts no slur on others.
PSALM 15:2-3 NIV

A perverse person stirs up conflict, and a gossip separates close friends.
PROVERBS 16:28 NIV

It often appears to us that there is nothing except our private walk with God which is more detested and assaulted by the devil that just this beautiful happy thing, the loyalty that is the basic quality of vital unity. We made one careful rule — the absent must be safe with us. Criticism, therefore, was taboo … what other way of life can satisfy the heart that is set on living in the ungrieved presence of its Lord? The very thought of Him shames unkindness.[2]

Amy Carmichael

These words express perhaps the most important antidote against gossip. Taking our eyes off ourselves — off of our own offenses, hurts, personal gripes, emotions, pride, and preferences — and fixing our gaze upon Him instead. When we remember how much He has sacrificed, how much He has given, how much He has suffered for us, criticizing and attacking each other seems utterly empty and foolish. He longs for us to love each other with a pure heart fervently. (See 1 Peter 1:22.) And this is how we demonstrate that we truly love Him — by *loving one another.* (See 1 John 4:20-21.) Gossip has no place in view of the Cross. And if we do not stray from the shadow of the Cross, our words will honor others — and our worthy King.

In Luke 6:45 Jesus tells us that out of the "abundance of the heart" the mouth speaks. And Psalm 19:14 says, "Let the words of my mouth, and the meditation of my heart be acceptable in Your sight, O Lord…" Obviously, the way that we think and the words that we speak go hand-in-hand. If we are not cultivating truth in our inner lives, we will not be able to speak truth-filled, life-giving words. But as we build our lives around Jesus Christ and His reality, our words will naturally reflect His truth and nature.

THIS WEEK

Read Proverbs 31:26:
She opens her mouth with wisdom, and on her tongue is the law of kindness.

Reflect: Have I ever asked God to fill my mouth with wisdom and the law of kindness? Am I willing to consecrate my tongue to be used for God's glory?

Read 1 Timothy 5:13:
And besides they learn to be idle, wandering about from house to house, and not only idle but also gossips and busybodies, saying things which they ought not.

Reflect: Have I been a gossip or busybody, saying or posting things that I ought not? Am I ready to repent and let God re-make this area of my life? What practical changes will that mean for my life?

Read Proverbs 16:28:
A perverse man sows strife, and a whisperer separates the best of friends.

Reflect: Have I been careless and unguarded with my tongue? Have my words ever brought discord among friends? Are there things God is asking me to make right in this area of my life?

Soul-Searching Questions
Am I willing to exchange meaningless chatter for purposeful edification? What conversations in my life are most in need of this change?

_____

_____

_____

_____

In what ways can I begin using my words to build others up instead of tearing them down?

Have I been speaking God's reality over my life, or words of negativity and doom? Do I need to renounce lies I have believed and embrace God's truth instead?

Knowing that I will give account for every idle word spoken, what would help me become more God-honoring with my words? Are there certain unhealthy influences that I should be avoiding?

Can I think of a time when someone spoke life and encouragement to me? How did it impact me? Are there specific people God is wanting me to encourage today?

Take it Deeper

The following resources have been selected to enhance your journey through this lesson and take these truths deeper into your heart.

Watch *The Power of the Tongue* a sermon by Eric Ludy available for free at Ellerslie.com.
Q. Have I ever fully realized the power of the tongue? What is God speaking to my heart about honoring Him and others with my words?

Listen to *Incorrigibly Cheerful* – a sermon by Eric Ludy available for free at Ellerslie.com.
Q. Does my heart-attitude towards my circumstances need to change so that I can express God's reality over my life? What can I meditate on throughout the week in order to better do this?

Other resources to take the message deeper:
Honorable Speech: How to Honor God and Others with Every Word You Speak – Online Course with Leslie Ludy

Week Nine

Friendship – Becoming a Faithful "Friend of the Bridegroom"

He who has the bride is the bridegroom; but the friend of the bridegroom, who stands and hears him, rejoices greatly because of the bridegroom's voice. Therefore this joy of mine is fulfilled.
JOHN 3:29

If I slip into the place that can be filled by Christ alone, making myself the first necessity to a soul instead of leading it to fasten upon Him, then I know nothing of Calvary love.[1]

Amy Carmichael

Keys to Being a Faithful Friend

1. Point Others to Jesus

If we seek to make another person emotionally dependent upon us rather than seeking to fasten them to Christ, **we become a barrier to their intimacy with Him**. The highest good that any person can ever find is not something that WE can offer, but is found only in Jesus Christ. Therefore our goal in every friendship or relationship should be to "fasten that soul to Christ" and not to ourselves.

We are called to be a reflection of Christ's love in our relationships, but we should never try to take first place in another person's heart. **That position must be reserved for Christ alone.**

...A man can receive nothing unless it has been given to him from heaven. You yourselves bear me witness, that I said, 'I am not the Christ,' but, 'I have been sent before Him.' He who has the bride is the bridegroom; but the friend of the bridegroom, who stands and hears him, rejoices greatly because of the bridegroom's voice. Therefore this joy of mine is fulfilled. He must increase, but I must decrease.
JOHN 3:27-31

While human counsel and encouragement have their place, God is first and foremost the One we should be pouring out our heart to – not our girlfriends. Let God become your primary sounding board and listening ear – He is a far better listener than any human ever could be.

*Trust in **Him** at all times ... pour out your hearts to **Him**, for **God** is our refuge.*
PSALM 62:8, EMPHASIS ADDED

When people come to you ... remember:
- It is not our job to have all the answers. We are only called to point them back to the only One who does.
- Instead of feeling that you must spend hours and hours listening to a person's tales of sorrow and woe and come up with a perfect answer to their question, encourage them to first and foremost take their cares to Him.
- Ask if they have truly laid their cares at Jesus' feet.
- Ask if they have truly searched the Word of God for specific answers to their situation.
- Ask if they have wrestled in prayer and cried out to God for their needs to be met.
- In many cases, they will have skipped those steps because they believe that their answers can be found in human wisdom or human comfort.

No matter how complicated a person's issues may be, **the root problem is still the same: sin. And the ultimate solution is still the same: Jesus Christ.**

If you are always the "counselor" or the "listening ear" then ask yourself whether you are truly exhorting people to take their cares to Jesus' feet.

It is not wrong to show empathy and to offer encouragement, but if you become someone's "first turn" that is when you know you need to be more proactive in fastening their soul to Christ.

2. Offer the Right Kind of Encouragement

> There is a kind of sympathy that weakens, and kind of sympathy that braces. Which of the two we have to offer depends on how much we know of the Spirit of our Lord. I have ceased to ask for easy ways for those I love most dearly. I ask instead for a conquering faith, for strength and the blessing of peace.[2]
>
> Amy Carmichael

We do not need to offer our friends a "poor you" message when they are facing difficult seasons. Our pity is not what they need. They need to tap into the amazing grace of God – that can enable them to do what they could never do in their own strength. Do not stand in the way of God's training ground in your friends' lives. Be their champion as they learn how to be strong in the Lord and become more than conquerors.

Here are some key verses to encourage others to rise up on God's strength:

> *Watch, stand fast in the faith, be brave, be strong.*
> 1 CORINTHIANS 16:13

> *…be strong in the Lord and in the power of His might.*
> EPHESIANS 6:10

> *And let us not grow weary while doing good…*
> GALATIANS 6:9

> *...endure hardship as a good soldier of Jesus Christ.*
> **2 TIMOTHY 2:3**

> *I can do all things through Christ who strengthens me.*
> **PHILIPPIANS 4:13**

3. Be Considerate of Others

Even our closest friendships should never make others feel overlooked or left out. Amy Carmichael wrote, "If … I seek to attach a friend to myself, so that others are caused to feel unwanted; if my friendships do not draw others deeper in [to Christ] then I know nothing of Calvary love."[3] Think of how much heartache could be avoided if we all lived by this principle throughout our lives! Most of us can remember the sting of being rejected or excluded when exclusive friendships formed around us in our childhood. And sadly, this happens all too often in adult friendships because of simple insensitivity. We must never forget that while Jesus shared a special connection with His disciples, He was never insensitive to the needs of the multitudes around Him – from the woman at the well to the little child who came to sit on His lap. I've learned that if I overlook the needs of those around me because I'm more concerned with enjoying certain "special friendships," I am not following Christ's example of selfless love.

4. Don't Fear Loneliness

If you truly seek to honor Christ in your friendships, you may find that you have fewer friends than other women have. Our culture teaches us to avoid loneliness at all costs. As a result we often compromise our spiritual beliefs in order to gain new friends or hold onto friendships we already have. But nothing is worth jeopardizing our relationship with Jesus Christ. Even if we have to walk through seasons of feeling very alone, He is worth it. And the Bible says that He wants to be our "All in all," especially in seasons of loneliness.

Practice going places on your own, ignoring your phone for an evening, shutting off your computer, and turning your gaze upon Jesus. Learn how to be "on your own with Jesus" and allow Him to show you that in His presence is the fullness of joy. And when you spend time with your friends, be sure that it is not something you look to or lean on as a primary source of happiness or security. Because truly, those things are found only in the truest Friend we will ever have.

5. Have Fun with Friends in a Christ-Honoring Way

Letting our spiritual guard down around our girlfriends often feels normal and justifiable. Our culture promotes this kind of self-indulgent behavior with the message, "Go ahead, let loose, have some fun, you deserve it!" The prevalent idea is that women today are under so much pressure in their daily lives (from family, work, society, etc.) that it is our "right" to get together with our girl friends and act however we want. Somehow following the cultural "girls' night" recipe of chick-flicks, gossip, food, and guy-talk (or some combination of the above) is supposed to relieve our stress and help us become better equipped to face our day-to-day challenges.

But does it?

Whenever I've been at a gathering of friends that was worldly and self-indulgent, I have always walked away feeling unsettled and agitated rather than refreshed and renewed. On the other hand, whenever I've spent time with women who truly honor God and others with their actions and conversations, I have been revived and strengthened.

The Bible warns against the behavior of certain women in the church who were "wandering about from house to house, and not only idle but also gossips and busybodies, saying things which they ought not" (1 Tim. 5:13). Sadly, this is an accurate picture of all too many Christian women's gatherings today, whether high-schoolers or middle-aged moms.

It's certainly true that spending time with our female friends can be a refreshing and wonderful experience. But it's all too easy to fall into the harmful patterns Scripture warns against if we are not purposeful about how we choose to spend our "girls' nights."

The culture may tell us that gossip, guy-talk, and self-indulgence are the best way to have fun with our girl friends, but God has an entirely different model – one that is refreshing, edifying, and truly strengthens us for the challenges of daily life.

Alternatives to Unhealthy Activities:

- Exchange Gossip for Encouragement
- Exchange Trivial Talk for Edifying Truth
- Exchange Chick Flicks for Real Life Christian Heroes

Godly friendships are a wonderful gift from our King. Let's begin seeking to honor Him in how we choose to use this gift. The world has its formula for enjoying time with our female friends – but His pattern is far better and more satisfying! When we invite Him to be the Guest of Honor at our girl-gatherings, we will come away uplifted, refreshed, and fulfilled!

Ointment and perfume delight the heart, and the sweetness of a man's friend gives delight by hearty counsel.
PROVERBS 27:9

WEEK 9: FRIENDSHIP

THIS WEEK

Read John 15:13:
Greater love has no one than this, than to lay down one's life for his friends.

Reflect: Do I approach friendships selfishly, or selflessly? In what practical ways can I follow Christ's example to lay down my life for my friends?

Read Ephesians 4:3:
Make every effort to keep the unity of the Spirit through the bond of peace. (NIV)

Reflect: Am I making every effort to keep godly unity and peace in my friendships? Are there practical things I can do in order to cultivate greater unity among my Christian brothers and sisters?

Read Matthew 7:12:
In everything, therefore, treat people the same way you want them to treat you, for this is the Law and the Prophets. (NASB)

Reflect: Am I walking according to this command in my friendships and family relationships? In what ways can I begin to live this out more effectively?

Soul-Searching Questions
Am I pointing others to Christ, or drawing them to myself? Are there specific ways in which I can begin to fasten my friends' souls to Jesus?

_____

_____

_____

_____

Have I been offering godly encouragement, or worldly encouragement? Am I a "friend of the Bridegroom" or am I slipping into the place that can be filled by Christ alone?

Am I considerate of others, or do any of my friendships cause others to feel unwanted? How can I better honor God in this area of my life?

Do I have an unhealthy dependence upon my friends? Am I willing to embrace loneliness and learn to lean on Christ alone?

Do I spend time with friends in a God-honoring way? What heathy activities can begin to replace unhealthy ones when I am with my friends?

Take it Deeper

The following resources have been selected to enhance your journey through this lesson and take these truths deeper into your heart.

Watch or Listen to *Pearl Farming* and *Grace for Dealing with People,* sermons from Eric Ludy available at Ellerslie.com.

Read *A God-Honoring Girls' Night* – an article by Leslie Ludy available at SetApartGirl.com. Q. What would you say is the focus of your get-togethers? How, if at all, does this need to change in order to become a time of true encouragement?

Listen to *People Pleasing – Wrong or Right?* – an episode of the Set Apart Girl Podcast at SetApartGirl.com. If you have trouble when it comes to saying *no*, overcommitting, or drawing the line between pouring out and taking time to refuel, give this a listen to become better equipped to being a life-giving friend.

Other resources to take the message deeper:
Christ-Centered Mentoring – Online Course with Leslie Ludy

Week Ten

Discernment – Overcoming Deception through Godly Wisdom

Hear instruction and be wise, and do not disdain it. Blessed is the man who listens to me, watching daily at my gates, waiting at the posts of my doors. For whoever finds me finds life, and obtains favor from the Lord.
PROVERBS 8:33-35

The Times in Which We Live

We live in a day and age where "righteousness stands at a distance; truth has stumbled in the streets, [and] honesty cannot enter" (Is. 59:14). Truth-centered, Christ-focused, biblically-sound believers are no longer commonplace; they have become the exception.

As set apart women living in such an era, we do not have the option of passively accepting anything and everything that is being dished out to us in the name of Christianity. Instead, God desires to equip us with the lost art of godly discernment. We must learn to clearly recognize the difference between truth and error, and proactively protect our souls against the enemy's insipid lies. Otherwise, we are in danger of becoming the "weak women" that Paul warns about in 2 Timothy 3:6: "For among them are those who enter into households and captivate weak women weighed down with sins…" (NASB).

"Captivate" in this verse means *to lead into captivity*. In other words, if we listen and agree with the deceitful voice of the enemy, we cannot be the bondservants of Christ because we have become enslaved to a lie. And "weak women" in this verse is a contemptuous term that means *silly and foolish*. We need only to study the fate of the "fool" mentioned frequently in Proverbs to learn the end result of choosing this destructive path!

But God has not left us to fend for ourselves amid all the confusion and deception that surrounds us today. He desires us to "come to the knowledge of the truth" (1 Tim. 2:4) even more than we desire it for ourselves. He does not intend us to spend our Christian lives being "tossed to and fro and carried about with every wind of doctrine, by the trickery of men, in the cunning craftiness of deceitful plotting" as it says in Ephesians 4:14.

Godly discernment is available for every one of us. But it doesn't just automatically come to us. We have a responsibility before God to *listen* to His voice, to *hear* His wisdom and *not disdain* it, to *watch* daily at His gates, and to *wait* at the posts of His doors. And He promises that if we seek His wisdom diligently, we *will* find it. (See Proverbs 8:17.)

Five Ways to Cultivate Godly Discernment

1. Beware of Itching Ears

> *For the time will come when they will not endure sound doctrine, but according to their own desires, because they have itching ears, they will heap up for themselves teachers; and they will turn their ears away from the truth, and be turned aside to fables.*
> 2 TIMOTHY 4:3-4

In this verse, "Itching ears" means *to be desirous of hearing something pleasant.* When we having itching ears, we no longer want to be molded and shaped by God's truth or convicted and refined by His Spirit. Instead, we try to modify His Word to align with our own ideas and desires, rather than let our ideas and desires come under submission to His Word.

There are many ear-tickling messages prevalent in the church today. Messages that exhort us to pursue our own happiness, fight for our own applause, cling to our own desires and wants, pattern our lives after the trends of pop-culture, treat sin with a wink and a chuckle, and make the Christian life all about *self* are a few of the most common ones. And often, these ear-tickling messages come in attractive packages. When a little bit of truth is carefully blended with an ear-tickling lie, it's easy to become convinced that it must be on-target, simply because it sounds so pleasant and right. Ear-tickling messages never bring us to a place of conviction, repentance, or brokenness over our sin. Instead, they merely help us put a spiritual label over our self-focused, sinful lives and provide us with a plethora of excuses for never needing to change or grow.

If you find yourself evaluating a message based on how it makes you feel or picking and choosing truth based on your personal preferences, you are an "itching ears" believer rather than a discerning one. So instead of asking, "How do *I feel* about this?" I encourage you to begin asking an entirely new question, "What does *God say* about this?"

2. Make God's Word Your Lifeline

There are so many devotionals, books, blogs, and Bible studies available to us that it's easy to turn to those things as our primary source of spiritual fuel. But nothing can replace His Word. It is meant to be "a lamp to [our] feet and a light to [our] path" (Ps. 119:105). If we are careless toward His Word, we will be susceptible to believing lies and error because our feet are not standing on the solid rock of His Truth. Now, more than ever, the Bible cannot be our casual companion; *it must become our lifeline*. We cannot regard God's Word as moldable to human opinions and ideas. We must find out what God says, and then build our lives upon that unshakable foundation. Christian books and resources certainly have value in a believer's life. But if we allow human thoughts to take the place of God's Word, our ability to discern truth from lies will be hindered.

Before you nod along with other Christians' ideas, stop and ask yourself some key questions: *Does this message agree with the truth of Scripture, not just on some points, but in its entirety? Do these thoughts and ideas align with God's nature and character?* If you are unsure, take time to seek answers in God's Word. Remember, He has promised that those who seek His wisdom diligently *will* find it!

> God's viewpoint is sometimes different from ours – so different that we could not even guess at it unless He had given us a Book which tells us such things.[1]
>
> Corrie ten Boom

3. Beware of "Trendy" Christianity

> When the Church and the world can jog comfortably together, you may be sure there is something wrong. The world has not altered. Its spirit is exactly the same as it ever was, and if Christians were equally faithful and devoted to the Lord, and separated from the world, living so that their lives were a reproof to all ungodliness, the world would hate them as much as it ever did.[2]
>
> Catherine Booth

Maybe you've noticed or been influenced by the "spiritual trends" that have been creeping into the Christian world; secular fads that have been adopted and spiritualized by modern believers. Here are just a handful of examples:

Trendy Evangelism: Don't be too aggressive in sharing your faith, don't act like you have all the answers, and don't make anyone feel badly about their sin. Instead, engage in philosophical conversations where no one is right or wrong, but everyone can feel heard and understood.

The Result: A church that is impotent in boldly sharing their faith and winning souls for Christ, while unbelievers remain comfortable and un-convicted over their sin.

Trendy Worship: Don't rely on simple, pure-hearted worship for church services and Christian gatherings. Instead, crank up the volume to deafening levels, put on an impressive show, and be sure to throw in a few popular secular songs for good measure.

The Result: A church that expects to be entertained instead of drawn into the holy presence of God — and maybe some long-term hearing loss as an added bonus.

Trendy Women's Ministry: Don't inhibit a woman from being whatever she wants, whenever she wants! Jesus was a feminist, and if you are a progressive Christian you'll be one too!

The Result: Christian women who are looking to the culture to define what real femininity is instead of to the One who created femininity in the first place.

Trendy Christian Relationships: Don't be guarded and discreet with what you share – the more "raw and real" the better! If you don't express every negative thought or emotion you feel, you aren't being authentic.

The Result: Christians who exalt their emotional baggage under the banner of "honesty" and who have forgotten how to be honorable or reverent in their communication.

Many of these spiritual trends in the church today are blended with just enough truth to make them confusing. For example, there is a healthy balance between boldly sharing your faith and simply taking time to listen and converse with an unbeliever. The problem is that many of us look at what is acceptable in the culture, and then adapt our Christian beliefs accordingly. It is *not* acceptable in today's world to be strong in what you believe – it's far more popular to take the "no one is right, we all have equally valid perspectives" approach. And when that kind of thinking creeps into our evangelism methods, our ability to win souls for Christ falls apart.

If you've ever wondered why Christianity today often seems powerless or mediocre, it's because Christianity and worldly thinking simply cannot mix. And when Christians try to blend popular, secular ideas into their faith, the church becomes little more than a spiritually-glossed-over social club.

4. Embrace the Old Paths

As consumer-driven Westerners, we are extremely drawn to anything new and trendy. We have been conditioned to seek after the "latest and greatest" when it comes to everything from technology to coffee drinks. And sadly, we often take this consumer mindset into spiritual things as well. Church leaders and Christian publishers are constantly scrambling to "give the customer what they want" by offering new and exciting bells and whistles to keep their consumer-driven audience interested.

One of the best ways you can avoid becoming just another "Christian consumer" is by approaching Christian events, church services, books, music, and resources with a new attitude. Instead of asking, "What am I getting out of this?" – we should be asking, "What is *God* getting out of this?" When our focus is on the glory of God rather than on feeding our own selfish wants, we won't chase after every new and trendy message that flashes through modern Christianity. Rather, we will esteem the "simplicity that is in Christ" (2 Cor. 11:3) – the uncomplicated, life-changing truth that doesn't need human bells or whistles to prop it up. "If *I* be lifted up," Jesus says, "I … will draw all men unto Me" (Jn. 12:32, emphasis added).

I encourage you to study the lives of men and women throughout Christian history who walked the "old paths" of simple, uncomplicated, powerful Christianity; men like Hudson Taylor, George Müller, D. L. Moody, R. A. Torrey, C. T. Studd, and Jim Elliot – and women like Catherine Booth, Elizabeth Fry, Amy Carmichael, Esther Ahn Kim, Corrie ten Boom, and Gladys Aylward. Their examples will inspire you toward one singular aim in your Christian walk – not to be entertained or catered to, but simply to *love and honor your worthy King*.

5. Understand God's Nature

As you fight to see the glory of God return to Christianity once again, never forget that *truth must always be delivered in a way that reflects God's nature*. Our quest for discernment can quickly turn into a haughty, demeaning attitude toward others if we are not guarded against human anger and pride. No matter how doctrinally sound or intellectually brilliant an idea may be, if it is marked by arrogance and self-seeking, God says it is *not* of Him: "This wisdom does not descend from above, but is earthly, sensual, demonic. For where envy and self-seeking exist, confusion and every evil thing are there" (Jms. 3:15-16).

As you seek to grow in godly discernment, be wary of clustering with believers who are impressive in doctrine but deficient in gentleness and love. Their arguments may be compelling and their grasp of Scriptural ideas dazzling, but if they are characterized by an ungracious attitude toward others, they are not operating in cooperation with the Spirit of God. *Never confuse discernment with a critical spirit.*

Beware of having a "zeal for God, but not according to knowledge" (Rom. 10:2) like many well-meaning Christians who, in their passion to fight for God's glory, look down on those they disagree with and treat them with contempt. Scripture tells us clearly, "the wrath of man does not produce the righteousness of God" (Jms. 1:20). It is not merely standing for the truth that matters, but standing for the truth *in God's way*.

Key Reminders for Such a Time as This

Become a discerning Christian in "such a time as this" can feel like a daunting task. But I'd like to leave you with two important thoughts.

1. Rely on God's grace.

Don't try to grow in godly wisdom by looking to your own efforts or willpower. Ask Him to equip you with the supernatural strength and wisdom you need to navigate the cloudy waters of modern Christianity. He can remove the fog of confusion and grant you a clear understanding of His truth — all you must do is ask.

2. Remember that Christianity, in a nutshell, is all about Jesus.

You may not yet have every hermeneutic tool mastered, every doctrinal notion refined, or every theological argument perfectly polished or figured out. (Maybe you don't even know what the word "hermeneutic" means!) Set your gaze upon Jesus Christ, and He will direct your steps. Reject messages that lead you away from Him, and embrace those that lead you into a fuller surrender to Him. If you fix your eyes upon Him, you will be "neither barren nor unfruitful in the knowledge of our Lord Jesus Christ" (2 Pet. 1:8).

Jude 1:24 leaves us with a wonderful promise: "Now to Him who is able to keep you from stumbling, and to present you faultless before the presence of His glory with exceeding joy…"

It is God alone who is able to keep us from stumbling. So let us offer ourselves fully to Him, holding nothing back, that He may lovingly shape us into lights that shine with His glory in the midst of a perverse and crooked generation. (See Philippians 2:15-16.)

THIS WEEK

Read 2 Timothy 3:6-7:
For among them are those who enter into households and captivate weak women weighed down with sins, led on by various impulses, always learning and never able to come to the knowledge of the truth (NASB).

Reflect: Am I a gullible woman, easily captivated by trendy messages? If so, what is causing this weakness in my life? What can I do, with God's help, to change this pattern and grow in true wisdom?

Read Psalm 119:105:
Your Word is a lamp to my feet and a light to my path.

Reflect: Do I know the Word of God? Am I allowing God's Word to be the guiding light of my life? In what practical ways can I deepen my understanding of His Word? How will knowing God's Word impact my ability to have discernment?

Read 2 Timothy 4:3-4:
For the time will come when they will not endure sound doctrine, but according to their own desires, because they have itching ears, they will heap up for themselves teachers, and they will turn their ears away from the truth, and be turned aside to fables.

Reflect: Do I have "itching ears"? Do I only like to hear messages that make me feel good? Am I willing to receive God's conviction and be corrected by Him? If not, am I willing for Him to make me willing? What are the dangers of being an "itching ears" believer?

Read Acts 17:11:
...[The Bereans] received the word with all readiness, and searched the Scriptures daily to find out whether these things were so.

Reflect: How did the Bereans reflect the attitude toward God's Word that I am called to have? Am I willing to eagerly search the Scriptures for truth just as they did?

Soul-Searching Questions

Am I earnestly seeking God's wisdom, or am I being tossed about by every wind and wave of doctrine? What would help me pursue God's wisdom and become less susceptible to deception?

Are there influences in my life — even in Christian circles — that are pulling me away from the rock-solid truth of God's Word? Am I reading books or listening to messages that cause me to doubt God or question His Word? What should I do about those influences?

Am I falling for any "trendy Christian messages"? How can I begin weighing every message against the Word of God? What does that mean practically? Which "trendy messages" is God challenging me to rethink?

Do I need to increase my memorization of Scripture so that I can keep God's Word hidden in my heart?

Take it Deeper

The following resources have been selected to enhance your journey through this lesson and take these truths deeper into your heart.

Watch *Betrayed with a Kiss,* a sermon by Eric Ludy available for free at Ellerslie.com. Allow God to show you whether you have fallen for any subtle error and replace those lies with His truth.

Other resources to take the message deeper:
The Set Apart Woman by Leslie Ludy (see chapter eight specifically: The Solid Rock)
Godly Discernment: Becoming a Woman of Wisdom – Online Course by Leslie Ludy

Week Eleven

Courage – Becoming Fearless for Such a Time as This

Strength and dignity are her clothing, and she smiles at the future.
PROVERBS 31:25 NASB

Have I not commanded you? Be strong and of good courage; do not be afraid, nor be dismayed, for the LORD your God is with you wherever you go.
JOSHUA 1:9

How To Become Fearless

1. Put on the Armor of God

James 4:7 says, "Resist the devil and he will flee from you." To become the valiant, set apart women we are called to be, we cannot just roll over and play dead when the enemy attacks us. We must stand firm and resist (in the mighty power of Christ's name), not allowing Satan to hinder God's purposes for our lives. As it says in Ephesians 6:10-11: "…be strong in the Lord and in the power of His might. Put on the whole armor of God, that you may be able to stand against the wiles of the devil."

Take some time to study what Scripture says about the nature of Christ versus the nature of Satan. Make a list of any of the attacks in your life that are coming from the enemy and not from God. Instead of accepting the harassment of the enemy, resist his attacks, standing confidently in the authority Jesus has given you. Once you recognize that you don't have to accept Satan's harassments and that Jesus Christ has given you power over forces of darkness, you can walk boldly and confidently in your position as a protected child of the King. (See Luke 10:19.)

2. Forsake the Worldly "Wisdom" of Fear

Our culture constantly bombards us with the message that being fearful is equivalent to being wise. However, living in fear is not the equivalent to living in wisdom. Rather, living in fear is living in direct disobedience to God. He doesn't just suggest that we "fear not." He commands us not to fear.

> *Have I not commanded you? Be strong and courageous. Do not be afraid; do not be discouraged, for the LORD your God will be with you wherever you go.*
> JOSHUA 1:9 NIV

> *…Sarah obeyed Abraham, calling him lord, whose daughters you are if you do good and are not afraid with any terror.*
> 1 PETER 3:6

We must begin to recognize fear for what it really is: sin.

Prayerfully ask God to awaken you to any areas of your life in which you are living in fear and self-protection, yet calling it wisdom. Ask Him to reshape your attitudes and habits in these areas. Practice turning to the Word of God instead of turning to worldly or ungodly counsel, and build your decisions around His wisdom instead of this world's. Instead of clinging self-protectively to your life, health, finances, and comforts, ask for the grace to completely entrust those areas of your life to Jesus Christ. When you do, you will discover a tremendous freedom from the bondage of fear.

3. Take Fearful Thoughts Captive

Martin Luther once wrote, "You can't stop the birds from flying over your head, but you can keep them from building a nest in your hair."[1] We may not be able to keep fearful thoughts from entering our minds, but we can kick them out the moment they arrive so that they don't take root inside our hearts and control our lives. That is the essence of 2 Corinthians 10:5, which says, "casting down arguments and every high thing that exalts itself against the knowledge of God, bringing every thought into captivity to the obedience of Christ."

Whenever you are tempted to dwell on fearful "what if" scenarios, fill your mind with truth instead. A great way to start this principle is by memorizing some of the Psalms. Some of my favorites are: Psalms 27, 34, 37, 46, 91, and 112. Whenever you are faced with temptation to fear, these words of truth can become vital weapons to chase away those thoughts. As you fill your mind with truth, lies will become more scarce.

Another strategy to overcoming fear and anxiety is to pray for someone else when the enemy harasses you with fearful thoughts. When we pray for someone else the focus shifts from ourselves and our own fears. This kind of prayer for others (also called intercessory prayer) turns us outward instead of inward.

When we know our God and believe Him to be exactly as His Word says He is, we have no reason to let fearful thoughts overtake our minds. Ask God for the strength to take authority over fearful thoughts. Train your mind to dwell upon His reality and His truth and develop the habit of immediately saying *no* to the enemy's foreboding suggestions.

The Secret of Our Spiritual Heroes

> The greatest old or new testament saints were on a level that is quite within our reach. The same spiritual power that enabled them to become our spiritual heroes, is also available to us.[2]
>
> **Goulburn**

All throughout the Bible, we are reminded that the *very same power* that enabled our spiritual heroes to accomplish mighty feats is also available to us. And not only that, but God specifically goes out of His way to make it clear that this conquering, bravehearted spirit is not only an important quality of godly masculinity, but a key component of godly femininity as well.

James 5:17 tells us, "Elijah was a man with a nature like ours, and he prayed earnestly that it would not rain; and it did not rain on the land for three years and six months." And Hebrews

6:12 says, "...do not become sluggish, but imitate those who through faith and patience inherit the promises."

For example, the chief characteristic that marks the life of the Proverbs 31 Woman is *strength*. Early in my Christian walk, I used to read the opening statement, "Who can find a virtuous [woman]?" (v.10) and picture a somber, mousy woman quietly sewing in a corner. Yet the Proverbs 31 woman is nothing of the kind! The word "virtuous" literally means *valiant, mighty, and strong*. It is the very same word used to describe King David's might when he wrestled the bear and lion, conquered Goliath, and slew tens of thousands of Israel's fiercest enemies.

Becoming a bravehearted woman does not come through striving, but through surrender. It is only when we lay down our own agenda at the foot of the Cross and yield to the supernatural enabling grace of God can we live out the high calling He has placed upon our lives. That is the secret of every true Christian hero. Becoming a bravehearted woman does not involve a complicated formula or an exhausting list of rules to follow. Rather it stems from a passionate devotion to the one true King, and a mighty faith in a mighty God.

Sprinting Toward the Battle

Our natural instinct is to run and hide from difficulty. We easily forget that God intends us to be spiritually *offensive*, not defensive. He has not called us to cower in a corner of fear and self-protection. Rather, He desires us to boldly go where others fear to go, that "out of weakness [we may be] made strong, [become] valiant in battle, [and turn] to flight the armies of the aliens" (Heb. 11:34).

It may sound like an impossible calling. But we must always remember that what God calls us to, He equips us for. It wasn't David who defeated Goliath. It was our mighty God who is altogether faithful and triumphant in every circumstance.

And just as He was victorious in those situations, He desires to show Himself victorious in our lives right now. So I encourage you to ask yourself: *What are the battles that God has called me to sprint toward today?*

Maybe it's accepting a task or assignment that intimidates you.

Maybe it's choosing to stand firmly in faith for a financial or physical need.

Maybe it's aggressively fighting for the salvation of a soul God has placed in your life.

Maybe it's choosing to conquer strongholds in your life such as fear or unforgiveness through enabling power of God.

Maybe it's joyfully embracing a challenging circumstance and trusting that God will gloriously triumph through it.

Whatever difficulties you have been shrinking back from, ask God to infuse you with a bravehearted spirit; one that will cause you to sprint toward the battle with liquid ferocity and absolute confidence in your mighty, faithful God.

God has called each of us to valiant femininity. By His grace, we can be set free from the snares of fear and anxiety, and filled with supernatural strength and courage that will cause the enemy to flee from us. God's strength puts us in a spiritually offensive position, instead of a defensive position. All we must do is allow Him to build us strong in Him and to dress us in His holy armor. Remember, "God has not given us a spirit of fear, but of *power and of love and of a sound mind*" (2 Tim. 1:7, emphasis added).

> Can not the same wonders be done now as of old? Do not the eyes of the Lord still run to and fro throughout the earth to show Himself strong on behalf of those who trust Him? …Where is now the Lord God of Elijah? He is waiting for Elijah to call on Him.[3]
>
> James Gilmour

THIS WEEK

Read 1 Peter 3:6:
…Sarah obeyed Abraham, calling him lord, whose daughters you are if you do good and are not afraid with any terror.

Reflect: Why is courage a key part of godly womanhood? Do I believe that God can cultivate His supernatural strength within me?

Read 2 Timothy 1:7:
For God has not given us a spirit of fear, but of power and of love and of a sound mind.

Reflect: Have I been thinking of myself as helpless against fear? Am I willing to renounce fear and receive God's gifts of love, power, and a sound mind?

Read James 4:7:
…Resist the devil and he will flee from you.

Reflect: Am I allowing Satan to harass me in any area of my life? Am I willing to obey God's command to resist him? Where does my power to resist him come from? What does that Bible say will happen if I resist him?

Soul-Searching Questions
Am I willing to lay down the "worldly wisdom" of fear and trust God with a childlike faith? How will this decision set me free from fear?

_____

_____

_____

_____

What battle is God asking me to sprint toward in His strength, just as David sprinted toward Goliath?

Do I believe that God has called me to be a woman of courage and valor? Am I ready to say *yes* to this call even if it takes me out of my comfort zone?

Am I willing to trust Him to do this work within me instead of attempting to conquer fear on my own?

Take it Deeper

The following resources have been selected to enhance your journey through this lesson and take these truths deeper into your heart.

Read *Gladys Aylward: The Little Woman* by Gladys Aylward with Christine Hunter.
Q. How did Gladys overcome fear and face incredibly dangerous situations with heavenly courage? What can I learn from her example of fearless living?

Listen to *The Immovable Soul* – a sermon by Eric Ludy available at Ellerslie.com.
Q. Is my life built upon the rock of God's Word or do I find myself easily shaken when trials, tests, and the unexpected presents itself in my life? How can I exchange flimsy faith for bedrock confidence in my God?

Listen to *Engaging in Spiritual Warfare* – a two-part series on the Set Apart Girl Podcast available at SetApartGirl.com.
Q. Prior to this message what was your understanding of spiritual warfare? What have you learned that you are desirous to practically apply to your life? What is your first step in being spiritually offensive rather than spiritually defensive?

Other resources to take the message deeper:
Fearless Living: How to Adopt a Battle Plan Against Anxiety – Online Course by Leslie Ludy

Week Twelve

Love – Discovering the Power of a Poured-Out Life

"…As the Father has sent Me, I also send you."
JOHN 20:21

[The virtuous woman] extends her hand to the poor, yes, she reaches out her hands to the needy … Strength and honor are her clothing; she shall rejoice in time to come.
PROVERBS 31:20, 25

It will be a happy day for England when Christian ladies transfer their attentions from poodles and terriers to destitute and starving children.[1]

Catherine Booth

Outward Living: A Key to Godly Womanhood

Proverbs 31 isn't just about the qualities of a virtuous woman. The first nine verses of the chapter are words from a mother to her son about the importance of forsaking trivial pursuits and taking up the cause of the weak and vulnerable. This godly woman exhorts her son: "Open your mouth for the speechless, in the cause of all who are appointed to die. Open your mouth, judge righteously, and plead the cause of the poor and needy" (Prov. 31:8-9). This is not just a calling for men. Throughout the rest of the chapter, the description of the Proverbs 31 woman is replete with images of sacrificial givenness and love toward the poor, weak, and needy.

The virtuous widow in 1 Timothy 5:10 is similar. This woman sets the pattern by which a godly woman should live, saying that she is "well reported for good works" and that her life has been marked by lodging strangers, washing the saints' feet, and relieving the afflicted. If you have been looking for clear purpose and focus in your life, don't overlook this sacred commission to become Christ's hands and feet to the weak, suffering, and lost.

Isaiah 58 describes God's "chosen fast" — a pattern of outward living that leads to joy, strength, healing, and protection:

> Is this not the fast that I have chosen … to share your bread with the hungry, and that you bring to your house the poor who are cast out; When you see the naked, that you cover him, and not hide yourself from your own flesh? **Then your light shall break forth like the morning, your healing shall spring forth speedily, and your righteousness shall go before you; the glory of the Lord shall be your rear guard.**
> ISAIAH 58:6-8, EMPHASIS ADDED

In our "look out for yourself" world, we need to understand that pleasing other people, serving other people, sacrificially giving to other people — when it's done in the *right* spirit and for the *right* reasons — is not dangerous or self-destructive. Rather, it is a joyful privilege and a crucial part of our calling.

How to Turn Outward

1. Understand the Call

> She extends her hand to the poor, yes, she reaches out her hands to the needy.
> PROVERBS 31:20

> …well reported for good works: if she has brought up children, if she has lodged strangers, if she has washed the saints' feet, if she has relieved the afflicted, if she has diligently followed every good work.
> 1 TIMOTHY 5:10

WEEK 12: LOVE

Pure and undefiled religion before God and the Father is this: to visit orphans and widows in their trouble, and to keep oneself unspotted from the world.
JAMES 1:27

"Not called!" did you say? "Not heard the call," I think you should say. Put your ear down to the Bible, and hear Him bid you go and pull sinners out of the fire of sin. Put your ear down to the burdened, agonized heart of humanity, and listen to its pitiful wail for help. Go stand by the gates of hell, and hear the damned entreat you to go to their father's house and bid their brothers and sisters, and servants and masters not to come there. And then look Christ in the face, whose mercy you have professed to obey, and tell Him whether you will join heart and soul and body and circumstances in the march to publish his mercy to the world.[2]

William Booth

God has prepared "good works" in advance for each of us to walk in. Ask Him to show you what that means for you today. It could be a simple as serving a needy neighbor or as grand as starting an orphanage overseas; as simple as sharing the Gospel with a co-worker or as grand as becoming a missionary to an unreached tribe. The key is to embrace the outward call that God has placed on your life, rather than thinking, *That's not for me – that's for someone else.*

Living a poured-out life starts with a new heart-attitude. One that says, "My life is no longer my own; I've been bought with a price. I'm ready to put aside selfish, shallow pursuits and make myself available to You, Lord, no matter the cost."

If you say *yes* to this sacred call and ask Him to lead you, you can be sure that your life will soon become the great adventure God intends it to be!

2. Understand the Need

- About 25,000 people die every day of hunger or hunger-related causes. (That's one person every three and a half seconds.)[3]
- There are between 143-163 million orphans in the world today, and the number is only growing.[4]
- There are 27 million human slaves in the world today; a large majority are young girls and women in forced prostitution.[5]
- There are nearly 700,000 children in the U.S. foster care system and nearly 80% of inmates serving time in U.S. prisons have come out of the foster care system.[6]
- Approximately 150,000 people die each day without knowing Christ — the biggest tragedy of all.[7]

It's hard to face these difficult statistics, but ignoring them is not the answer. I encourage you to purposefully take time every week to set aside frivolous activities — such as mindlessly surfing the Internet or meandering around social media pages — and instead begin learning about the needs around the world and in your own community. Ask God to give you His heart and burden for these lives, and show you if there is one particular step He is asking you to take in order to become His hands and feet to this dying world.

3. Turn Your Eyes Upon Jesus

Ask God to turn your eyes upon Jesus. Spend time in His presence and in His Word and begin building your thoughts around Him — not the things of this world. And soon, as Lilias Trotter once wrote, a strange "dimness" will come over all that is apart from Him.[8] Nothing else will matter anymore but the things that are eternal. That is how we know our lives are rightly focused.

4. Receive His Enabling Grace

If embracing an outward life feels impossible, remember that God never asks us to do anything that He is not prepared to equip us for. If we try to serve in our own strength, we will fall on our face. But if we serve in His strength, the world can be changed … one life at a time.

Amy Carmichael once wrote about God being a "very present help in trouble" – so present, in fact, that even a whisper will bring the help that we need in the moment. "Do you need courage? All you must do is whisper, 'Thy courage, Lord!' and it will come. Do you need patience? Just whisper, 'Thy patience, Lord!' and it will come – not tomorrow, but right now."[9] That is what it means to tap into God's enabling grace. Remember, grace is so much more than the "hug" or favor of God. It is supernatural strength for the impossible life to which we are called. Receiving God's grace begins with an attitude that says, "Lord, I can't – but *You* can!"

Never forget, "Faithful is He that calleth you, who also will do it" (1 Thes. 5:24 KJV).

THIS WEEK

Read James 2:14-17:

What does it profit, my brethren, if someone says he has faith but does not have works? Can faith save him? If a brother or sister is naked and destitute of daily food, and one of you says to them, "Depart in peace, be warmed and filled," but you do not give them the things which are needed for the body, what does it profit? Thus also faith by itself, if it does not have works, is dead.

Reflect: Am I positioning myself to be Christ's hands and feet to those in need? Do I need to pour out my life on behalf of others in greater measure?

Read Matthew 25:34-40:

Then the King will say to those on His right hand, 'Come, you blessed of My Father, inherit the kingdom prepared for you from the foundation of the world: for I was hungry and you gave Me food; I was thirsty and you gave Me drink; I was a stranger and you took Me in; I was naked and you clothed Me; I was sick and you visited Me; I was in prison and you came to Me … inasmuch as you did it to one of the least of these My brethren, you did it to Me.'

Reflect: Have I been serving others as unto Jesus? Have my motives for serving been wrong? In what ways can I more purposefully love Christ by sacrificially loving others?

Soul-Searching Questions

In what ways do I feel God is asking me to reach out to the weak and vulnerable on His behalf?

WEEK 12: LOVE

What is a practical step I can take this week toward living a poured-out life?

How will turning outward bring lasting joy and fulfillment into my life?

Have I been living selfishly? Am I willing to get out of my comfort zone in order to show selfless love to others?

Take it Deeper

The following resources have been selected to enhance your journey through this lesson and take these truths deeper into your heart.

Watch *Depraved Indifference* – a short film available at Ellerslie.com.
Q. What is God speaking to your heart through this challenging message?

Listen or watch *The Perilous Mission* – a sermon by Eric Ludy available at Ellerslie.com.
Q. In what ways have I turned a blind eye to the persecuted church? In what ways can I remember those who are suffering for Christ's name as being bound with them? (See Hebrews 13:3.)

Other resources to take the message deeper:

True Happiness: How to Exchange Temporal Distractions for Lasting Contentment – Online Course with Leslie Ludy

Practical Poured-Out Living – an article by Leslie Ludy available at SetApartGirl.com

Given: A Journey Into Orphan Work – a two-part article series by Annie Wesche available at SetApartGirl.com

Appendix

Cleaning Out the Sanctuary

Search me, O God, and know my heart: try me and know my thoughts: and see if there be any wicked way in me, and lead me in the way everlasting.
PSALM 139:23 KJV

This guide is meant to be a helpful tool to assist you in the process of cleaning out your sacred sanctuary. Please do not begin this process unless you have plenty of time in which to work through it. This is a process that demands an extended, focused effort. You shouldn't feel rushed, but should slowly and thoughtfully walk your way through these questions. Make sure you have a pen and paper ready to make note of that which the Spirit of God what the Spirit of God stirs within your heart and mind.

This will certainly not be an exhaustive process. There could likely be other things not mentioned in the lists below that have muddied the walls of your sanctuary. As you journey through the following questions, allow the Spirit of God to bring things to your mind not included in this list as well. Our God is faithful not to leave any stone unturned. He jealously longs for your sanctuary to be purified and readied for intimacy with Him.

Let me forewarn you that this process is not easy. When a cyst is removed from the body, a knife is involved. As the knife of the Spirit of Christ is inserted into our hearts, the pain at times will be extreme, but the freedom that follows is ten million times worth the momentary struggle within your heart and mind. Your Prince desires to take your trembling hand and walk you through this process of purification. Invite God's Holy Spirit to penetrate into the deepest caverns of your heart and show you what must be done to gain unhindered intimacy with your Prince.

Getting the Most out of this Process

When you have lived in the midst of trash for so long you accustom yourself to its presence, and no longer realize that it is there. It is similar to hanging out in a smelly barn. If you are in the barn long enough you no longer realize how badly it stinks. If this is the first time you have ever walked through a cleaning process like this, it can be quite shocking to realize how much junk you have allowed to pile up inside your life. Hold tightly to your Prince's hand throughout the process and remember His amazing love for you. He loves you so much that He can't allow you to remain buried beneath the trash.

With each of these questions you will need to answer *yes* or *no*. There is no use hiding from the truth and acting as if the question doesn't apply to you if it really does. God already knows every thought, action, and attitude you have ever had throughout your entire existence. Trying to justify or reason the garbage away doesn't remove it. If trash is there, it is there. Only by answering honestly can you remove the garbage from your sanctuary and discover the freedom that Christ purchased for you on the Cross.

If you answer *yes*, you will be acknowledging that you have violated your relationship with Christ in that specific area. It is important then, that you walk through the following five steps of dealing with that specific sin before God.

Five Steps to Freedom

1. **Humbly tell God about the specific sin that comes to your mind.** Yes, He already knows, but speaking it to God brings it to the surface so that He is able to remove it from your sanctuary. Acknowledging your specific sin to God is like saying, "God, I finally get it! I agree with You! This was wrong!"

2. **Ask forgiveness from God.** It's only when we first acknowledge the sin and then ask Him to wash us clean, based on the merits of His shed blood, that the cleansing really can take place. It is at that moment that we ask for and receive His forgiveness that we really are washed clean.

3. **Turn and walk a new and different way.** The Bible calls it repentance. It simply means deciding to no longer do that sin again. This is not just a feeling of remorse for our sin, it's a practical change of our life so that we don't allow that sin to find its way back into our sacred sanctuary ever again.

4. **Ask God to show you if anything else needs to be done about your specific sin.** If your wrongdoing affected someone else, it is possible that God may want you to go to them and make things right. If you stole you may need to repay with interest. If you lied then you may need to set the record straight by telling the truth and attempting to undo the effects of your lie as much as possible. If you were playing with witchcraft, then you maybe need to burn the items associated with your witchcraft.

    IMPORTANT: There are a few exceptions to this step. If your specific sin involved something that you harbored in your mind like lust, jealousy, or anger – then it typically is NOT an appropriate thing to confess those particular sins to the target of your wrong thoughts.

    Remember though, that there isn't a formula for making wrongs right. That is why we must go to God and say, "God, I'm willing to do whatever I need to do to make this right – so please show me what I need to do." It's a hard prayer to pray, but if we willingly allow God to direct us, it is amazing how radically our life can be changed in even a short period of time. Sometimes God may want you to do something large to make right what you wronged, but other times His requests may be as simple as beginning to show the love of Christ to someone in a practical way.

5. **Obey what God leads you to do.** When you say to God that you are willing to do whatever it takes to make things right, then when He communicates that You need to do something – do it!

    NOTE: If you sense that God wants you to deal with an individual who was impacted by your sin and/or that He desires you to confess your sin to a Christian teammate, then read the following two "Freedom Tools" on the next page, for some assistance in the process.

Freedom Tool #1: Dealing with Those Impacted by Your Sin

If God asks you to personally interact with the individual you wronged then there are three things that are important to remember. First, express sincere regret over your wrongdoing when you acknowledge it to them. Secondly, sincerely and humbly apologize and ask their forgiveness for what you did (and don't make your request for forgiveness conditional upon them forgiving you — it is possible that they may not). And thirdly, do whatever it takes to make right what you have done wrong. It is not always possible to right what you have wronged, but oftentimes there are things you can do (whether small or large) to express the love of Christ in a situation or a relationship where you originally displayed the absence of Christ.

Freedom Tool #2: Dealing with a Christian Teammate

If God leads you to confess your sin(s) to a Christian teammate, then there are two things that are important to remember. First, if other people participated in your wrongdoing, then be careful not to dishonor them or injure them in your personal confession of sin. You are responsible for your behavior and the other participants are responsible for theirs. Secondly, be willing to appear weak in your teammate's eyes. Often, your example of honesty and weakness can be a heavenly invitation for your teammate to follow so that they too are able to gain ground in their own spiritual life. It can be extremely difficult at times to share your weaknesses with your teammates, but the process of overcoming the sin, and being freed from the sin, often demands it.

NOTE: If you don't yet have a person, or a small group, in your life to whom you are accountable, then I would encourage you to begin asking God to provide you with a Christian teammate that you can come to with your struggles and victories. Teammates are a vital tool for spiritual success.

Part One: Removing the Smelly Garbage

Let's get started. Remember to take this process slowly. Even if it takes you a week to make it through, it is better to have "quality" in this experience than it is to have "quickness." Trash within our sanctuary takes on four different appearances. They are as follows:

1. Sinful acts you committed
2. Christlike acts you did *not* commit
3. Sinful thoughts/attitudes you had
4. Christlike thoughts/attitudes you did *not* have

Let's work through each of these separately.

Sinful Acts You Committed:

For each of these questions it is important that you write down every incident that comes to your mind so that you can deal with each incident individually. Since each sin was committed individually, each sin must also be dealt with individually. Throughout the process allow the Holy Spirit to bring back to your mind even things that happened when you were a child. NOTE: For each sin the Holy Spirit brings to your attention, be sure to walk through the "Five Steps to Freedom" process detailed on pages 126-127.

Question 1: Have you ever deliberately passed around lies about someone in order to injure them?

Question 2: Have you ever gossiped? Have you ever exposed someone's faults for the pure enjoyment of seeing them look bad or odd in someone else's eyes?

Question 3: Have you ever made someone feel less important because of how they dressed, how they spoke, how little money they had, the color of their skin, or because they were unable to help you?

Question 4: Have you ever made someone feel more important simply because of how they dressed, how they spoke, how much money they had, the color of their skin, or because of their ability to help you?

Question 5: Have you ever hurt someone by the way you spoke to them or by the way you treated them? Have you ever, whether verbally or physically, harmed someone out of anger or frustration?

Question 6: Have you ever taken revenge on someone for something they did to you? Have you ever "evened the score" by harming someone's life or reputation in some way?

Question 7: Have you ever fought with someone, whether verbally or physically, with the intent to hurt them?

Question 8: Have you ever participated in the taking of life – whether through having an abortion, consenting for another to have an abortion, counseling someone towards suicide, or through the act of deliberately (or accidentally) committing murder?

Question 9: Have you ever cheated on a test? Have you ever passed on false information about yourself to look better in someone's eyes?

Question 10: Have you ever counted something incorrectly, or measured something inaccurately for the purpose of personal gain?

Question 11: Have you ever participated in sexual banter, flirtation, or dirty talk? Have you ever attempted to sexually arouse another person with your speech or physical behavior outside of marriage?

Question 12: Have you ever willfully participated in any mode of sexual touch with another person outside of marriage? Have you ever willfully allowed someone to sexually arouse you? Have you ever touched or observed someone else for the purpose of your own sexual arousal? Have you ever touched or observed someone else for the purpose of sexually arousing them?

Question 13: Have you ever willfully been aroused, or aroused someone else to the point of sexual climax outside of marriage?

Question 14: Have you ever willfully engaged sexually with an object, animal, or anything else outside of the opposite sex? Have you ever willfully engaged sexually with a member of your same sex?

Question 15: Have you ever been immodest? Have you ever allowed sensuous portions of your body to be observable by men? Have you ever deliberately dressed in a manner that you knew would cause a man to be sexually aroused? Have you allowed your body to be viewed in a manner that would make your husband or future husband jealous?

Question 16: Have you ever broken a trust? Have you ever (knowingly or unknowingly) shared something that you promised never to reveal? Have you ever violated a person's trust by doing something that you were asked (or you promised) not to?

Question 17: Have you ever deliberately said, written, or implied something that was not true for your own selfish gain or for the selfish gain of someone else? Have you ever exaggerated the truth or diminished the truth for your own selfish gain or for the selfish gain of someone else?

Question 18: Have you ever lied to your parents or to anyone else, for the purpose of covering up your sinful behavior or for the purpose of protecting your image?

Question 19: Have you ever dishonored your parents? Have you ever shared something about your parents with the intent to lower their reputation in someone else's eyes? Have you ever diminished their character by behaving poorly in public?

Question 20: Have you ever dishonored an authority figure (teacher, police officer, coach, pastor/youth pastor, political official, etc.)? Have you ever shared something about an authority figure with the intent to lower their reputation in someone else's eyes? Have you ever diminished their character by behaving poorly in public while you were representing them?

Question 21: Have you ever been disobedient to your parents? Has there ever been a time when your parents asked you to do something and you either did not obey or you were slow to obey?

Question 22: Have you ever been disobedient to God? Has there ever been a time when God was asking you to do something and you either did not obey or you were slow to obey?

Question 23: Have you ever stolen? Have you ever taken something from someone else's possession (whether large or small) that you did not buy, were not given, or had not temporarily borrowed with the owner's permission?

Question 24: Have you ever willfully consumed a substance, be it alcohol or a drug, making yourself subservient to its mind-controlling powers for the purpose of social acceptance?

Question 25: Have you ever bragged about yourself? Have you ever made mention of your personal accomplishments or your abilities to others for the purpose of looking better in their eyes?

Question 26: Have you ever participated in any evil practices or rituals that honored any other power other than Jesus Christ, the God of the Bible? Have you ever allowed another power, outside that of God's Holy Spirit, to work through you, speak to you, direct you, or inform you in any way?

Question 27: Have you ever misused God's name? Have you ever behaved in public in any way that would disgrace the name of Jesus Christ? Have you ever spoken in such a manner that the person of Jesus Christ was lessened in others' eyes?

Christlike Acts You Did *Not* Commit

For some of these questions it is not possible to write down each individual incident. For the ones you answer yes to but are unable to remember individual incidents, follow steps 1, 2, and 3 from the "Five Steps to Freedom" process detailed on pages 126-127. When you are able to remember individual incidents, be sure to write each of the individual incidents down and walk through each of the five steps.

Question 28: Have you not allowed Christ (God's Word) to be the determining factor in how you make decisions and live your life, and have you instead trusted in your own reasoning abilities?

Question 29: Have you ever been ungrateful? Has there ever been anything that you have been given, by either another person or by God, throughout your lifetime for which you did not properly show or express gratitude?

Question 30: Have you ever been stingy with your possessions? Have you ever been exposed to a person's need, had the resources to help them, but chose not to?

Question 31: Have you ever been unhelpful? Have you ever been exposed to someone in need of assistance, been in a position to help them, but chose not to?

Question 32: Have you ever given in to unbelief? Have you ever been in a situation where you allowed your mind to be controlled by fear, anxiety, and foreboding, rather than turning to God, asking for His assistance, and trusting that He is faithful to supply everything you need?

Question 33: Have you ever given in to impatience? Have you ever given up on something you were asked to do, simply because the process was either too difficult or not going fast enough? Have you ever complained about a wait being too long?

Question 34: Have you ever been unkind? Have you ever been in a situation where you noticed someone that was in need of kindness, but for the sake of your own comfort or reputation, you ignored them?

Question 35: Have you ever had the opportunity to share the truth of Jesus Christ, but for the sake of your own comfort or reputation, you ignored it?

Question 36: Have you failed to honor your husband/future husband in the way you have chosen to live your life? If your spouse/future spouse was able to watch your life, know your every thought, and see how you protect your heart, would he feel jealous, hurt, and unloved by your actions? If he were able to see you interact with other men, would he feel as though you were giving away something that was meant to be only his?

Question 37: Have you been unwilling to give your every possession over to Jesus, so that no longer are you an owner, but now you are a steward of them? Have you been unwilling to allow Him to reconstruct your daily schedule to make time with Him the most important thing on the agenda? Have you been unwilling to give Him complete access to your bank account? Have you been unwilling to fully entrust Him with Your future? Have you been unwilling to give Him all your rights (i.e. the right to be married, the right to be comfortable and happy, and the right to do things your way)?

Sinful Attitudes/Thoughts You Had

Similar to the last section, for some of these questions it is not possible to write down each individual incident. For the ones you answer yes to but are unable to remember individual incidents, follow steps 1, 2, and 3 from the "Five Step to Freedom" process detailed on pages 126-127. When you are able to remember individual incidents, be sure to write each of the individual incidents down and walk through each of the five steps.

Question 38: Have you ever had jealous thoughts? Have you ever wanted something for yourself that really wasn't yours, and were jealous when someone else enjoyed it?

Question 39: Have you ever wanted to switch lives with someone else? Have you ever been mentally consumed by the longing to have something of material value that belongs to someone else?

Question 40: Have you ever complained? Have you ever given in to self-pity?

Question 41: Have you ever been fearful of the future? Have you ever convinced yourself that bad things will take place in the next weeks, months, and/or years of your life?

Question 42: Have you been unforgiving? Do you have anyone in your life that you have either never forgiven or refused to forgive?

Question 43: Have you allowed resentment and bitterness (towards God or another person) into your heart and mind?

Question 44: Have you ever allowed your mind to dwell on thoughts that were untrue, perverted, impure, proud, or selfish? Have you allowed your mind to be unguarded, where your thoughts were not checked and filtered, but free to infect your inner world?

Question 45: Have you ever had hateful thoughts towards God or another person?

Question 46: Have you ever given in to anger and entertained thoughts of destruction toward someone you were angry with?

Question 47: Have you ever felt more important than others? Have you ever thought of anyone as being less important than you?

Christlike Attitudes/Thoughts You Did *Not* Have

Similar to the last two sections, for some of these questions it is not possible to write down each individual incident. For the ones you answer yes to but are unable to remember individual incidents, follow steps 1, 2, and 3 from the "Freedom Steps to Freedom" process detailed on pages 126-127. When you are able to remember individual incidents, be sure to write each of the individual incidents down and walk through each of the five steps.

Question 48: Have you ever felt apathetic, uninterested, and/or unloving towards those who do not yet know Jesus Christ?

Question 49: Have you ever felt apathetic, uninterested, and/or unloving towards those who are your Christian brothers and sisters?

Question 50: Have you been unwilling to sacrifice out of your personal resources to support those less fortunate than you?

Question 51: Have you been unwilling to look like a fool in order to serve the Lord Jesus Christ?

Question 52: Have you been unwilling to be mistreated, ridiculed, mocked, and falsely accused in order to serve the Lord Jesus Christ?

Question 53: Have you been unwilling to make God's opinion of you more important than the world's opinion?

Part Two: Kicking Out the "Other Lovers"

Kicking out "other lovers" can be a little more challenging than "removing the smelly trash." This is due to the simple reason that garbage is something that stinks, while "other lovers" are things that we, as humans, secretly enjoy. As you walk through the following process, you will begin to realize that there could be some very unhealthy things taking up residence within your sanctuary. Some of these "other lovers" can be yanked out like a weed, but there may be others that will take some time, and potentially some help from some mature Christians on the outside, to fully remove them from the soil of your heart. (I call these "tree-stump" issues.)

There are five categories of "other lovers" that we will need to go through. They are the following:
- Romantic attachments
- Addictive behaviors
- Unforgiveness
- Inordinate affections
- Ungodly allurements

Let's work through each of these separately.

Romantic Attachments

Romantic attachments are an insidious thing. We derive tremendous pleasure from them for a season, but long after the fling is over we find that these romantic attachments have glued themselves to our souls and refuse to leave our heart and imagination. For years they can toy with our emotions, pluck at our heartstrings, distract us from our Heavenly Prince, as well as hinder our ability to give ourselves completely to our earthly husband. If you have ever participated in any of the following emotionally-based activities outside of marriage, then it is very possible that you have a romantic attachment taking up space within your sacred sanctuary and you need to kick it out.

"Weed-Level" Attachments

If you have participated in any of the three following activities then carefully walk through steps 1, 2, and 3 of the "Five Steps to Freedom" process detailed on pages 126-127. Ask the Holy Spirit to remove any existing attachments and free you from their hold.

- If you ever cultivated a mental infatuation toward another person
- If you ever nurtured romantic affections toward another person other than a fiancé or husband
- If you were ever sexually aroused by another person's words or physical touch

Tree-Stump-Level" Attachments

If you have participated in any of the four following activities then it may be necessary to involve a biblical counselor in the process of removing these "other lovers" from the soil of your heart. The more that is given of yourself in a sensually-based relationship, the stronger the hold the romantic attachment can have on your heart. First walk through steps 1,2, and 3 of the "Five Steps to Freedom" process detailed on pages 126-127, then if you sense that a more aggressive tact is necessary, seek out someone who can help walk you through the removal process on a deeper, more personalized level. NOTE: In some situations God may also lead you to walk through steps four and five to deal with the romantic attachment. If so, it may be important to gain advice from a biblical counselor before you do.

- If you ever spoke words of commitment towards another person
- If you ever had words of commitment spoken towards you by another person
- If you ever reached sexual climax with the assistance of another person
- If you participated in repeated sexual encounters with another person

Addictive Behaviors

Addictive behaviors provide us with comfort and security, and therefore can be a challenge to remove. When you develop an addictive behavior, you often don't even realize it. You justify its presence in your life with makeshift rationalizations. You tell yourself things like, *This is something that everyone does*, or *I could give it up anytime I want to*, or *After all, doesn't God want me to be happy and/or successful*? The tell-tale sign of an addictive behavior is that it is nearly impossible to let go of it. Addictive behaviors take up space in our sacred sanctuary because they provide a false sense of comfort and security, causing us to not allow Christ to provide us with the real thing. Anything that attempts to replace the work of Christ within your life is a hindrance from you discovering the fullness of an intimate relationship with Him. Addictive behaviors, even the seemingly small and insignificant ones, must be kicked out. You will find that some of the things listed below are not sinful in and of themselves, it is the unhealthy and controlling craving for them that is sinful.

"Weed-Level" Addictions

If you answer yes to any of the five following questions then carefully walk through steps 1, 2, 3, and 5 of the "Five Steps to Freedom" process found on pages 126-127, When you pray both individually and with your Christian teammate, ask the Holy Spirit to powerfully break the unhealthy and controlling hold that the addiction has over your life.

Has your personal sense of need for energy and alertness created an unhealthy and controlling craving for any of the following items: Caffeine, painkillers, diet supplements, or performance enhancers?

Has your personal sense of need to look perfect physically created an unhealthy and controlling craving for any of the following activities: Excessive physical exercise, daily weight observance, inordinate amounts of time in front of the mirror, or a mental preoccupation with what is wrong with your body and how it could possibly be improved?

Has your personal sense of need for a "break from reality" created an unhealthy and controlling craving for any of the following activities: Television and movies, excessive sleeping, book/magazines, daydreaming, or listening to music?

Has your personal sense of need for being "popular" and for being "part of the action" created an unhealthy and controlling craving for any of the following activities: Being where the party is, always being around friends, always being active, always knowing the latest gossip, always being the center of attention, or doing whatever it takes to be considered popular?

Has your personal sense of need for being "taken care of" and "comfortable" created an unhealthy and controlling craving for any of the following items: Money, clothes, jewelry, expensive brand names, or the compulsive use of credit card debt to obtain them?

"Tree-Stump-Level" Addictions

If you answer yes to any of the following five questions then it may be necessary to involve a biblical counselor, and in many cases a medical doctor, in the process of removing these "other lovers" from the soil of your heart. First walk through steps 1, 2, 3, and 5 of the "Five Steps to Freedom" process found on pages 126-127, then if you sense that a more aggressive tact is necessary, seek out someone who can help walk you through the removal process on a deeper more personalized level.

Has your personal sense of need for "emotional validation" and "sensual expression" caused you to have a controlling craving for any of the following activities: Sharing sexual contact with another person, experiencing sexual arousal to a point of climax, having sexual imaginings, or viewing pornography?

Has your personal sense of need to look perfect physically caused you to have a controlling craving for any of the following activities: Maintaining your figure as a bulimic, or maintaining your figure as an anorexic? If you answer *yes*, medical attention is essential.

Do you have a dislike for yourself that causes you to have a controlling craving for any of the following activities: Personal harm through bulimia or anorexia (if yes, medical attention is essential) personal harm through cutting or self-mutilation (if yes, biblical counseling is essential, and medical attention is highly advised), or personal harm through returning to an abusive relationship (if yes, biblical counseling is essential)?

Do you have an emotional sickness that causes you to have a controlling craving for any of the following activities: Displays of anger and/or violence, purposeful depression to allow self-pity to have its way, or deliberate physical sickness?

Do you have a controlling craving to participate in any of the following activities: Excessive eating, nicotine intake, drug use (legal or illegal), or alcohol use?

Unforgiveness

Unforgiveness is our way of punishing those that have hurt us. We reason that if we hate them, think evil thoughts about them, resent them, and turn bitter against them, that we will somehow get back at them for all the horrible things that they did to us. Ironically, unforgiveness rarely accomplishes what we think it accomplishes. Typically the only thing that happens is the disease of unforgiveness eats away at our insides and turns our souls black with hate. Unforgiveness works like a blockade against the work of Christ within our lives. It paralyzes us within almost like we have prison chains on our ankles and wrists. For a healthy spiritual life, it is essential that we learn how to walk through the process of forgiving someone who has hurt us. Forgiveness is one of the critical avenues by which Christ increases in our life. If we block off that avenue with unforgiveness, it disables us from experiencing life-changing intimacy with our Prince in our sacred sanctuary.

One of the reasons why many of us struggle with the forgiveness process is we have a misunderstanding of what forgiveness is. Most of us think that to forgive someone is to *forget* what they did, excuse their wrong, and to "let them off the hook." But forgiveness is a very different process than that. Instead of forgetting, excusing, and "letting them off" it is rather a radical freeing of the soul involving three critical decisions of the will.

Three Critical Decisions of the Will

1. **Choosing to take their "hook" out of you.** *(Making a choice for peace instead of bitterness. Agreeing to live, from this point on, with any practical consequences of their sin against you,*

and allowing God, in the way only He can, to transform the "wrong" that was done to you into something that leads you closer to Him.)

2. **Choosing to let them off your "hook."** *(Being willing to see God save, forgive, and heal them. Choosing, from this point on, not to hold the "wrong" they did to you against them.)*

3. **Choosing to put them on God's "hook."** *(Allowing God to be the one to deal with them for the "wrong" they committed against you.)*

"Weed-Level" Unforgiveness

If you answer yes to any of the four following questions then, for each of the instances and/or individuals involved, carefully walk through both the "Three Critical Decision of the Will" (just mentioned above) and the "Five Steps to Freedom" process detailed on pages 126-127. As you walk through this emotionally charged process, allow yourself to be honest with your feelings. Ask the Holy Spirit to assist you in taking these very important steps forward in your spiritual life.

Are you harboring unforgiveness against anyone outside of your family for doing any of the following things to you: For stealing something of material value from you, for treating you rudely, for ignoring you, for forgetting you, for accidentally injuring you, for verbally abusing you, for lying to you, for gossiping about you, for making you wait, for embarrassing you, for cutting you off, for not assisting you when you needed help, or for not showing gratitude to you for something you did to help them?

Are you harboring unforgiveness against a family member for doing any of the following things to you: For stealing something of material value from you, for rudely treating you, for ignoring you, for causing you discomfort, for forgetting you, for accidentally injuring you, for lying to you, for gossiping about you, for making you wait, for embarrassing you, for not assisting you when you needed help, or for not showing gratitude to you for something you did to help them?

Are you harboring unforgiveness against yourself for doing any of the following things: For not being good enough, smart enough, beautiful enough, talented enough, healthy enough, likable enough, or confident enough?

Are you blaming God, and therefore harboring unforgiveness against Him, for doing any of the following things: For not making you smart enough, beautiful enough, talented enough, healthy enough, likable enough, or confident enough? Or for not giving you a better family?

"Tree-Stump-Level" Unforgiveness

Due to the nature of "Tree-Stump-Level" Unforgiveness, if you answer yes to any of the four following questions then the assistance of a biblical counselor in the "forgiveness" process is highly advised. For each of the instances and/or individuals involved, carefully walk through both the "Three Critical Decision of the Will" (just mentioned on page 141-142) and the "Five Steps to Freedoms" process detailed on pages 126-127. As you walk through this emotionally charged process, allow yourself to be honest with your feelings. Ask the Holy Spirit to assist you in taking these very important steps forward in your spiritual life.

Are you harboring unforgiveness against anyone outside or inside of your family for doing any of the following things to you: For intentionally injuring you, for falsely accusing you, for betraying an intimate trust, or for sexually violating you (i.e. abuse, rape, touching, looking, or taking advantage)?

Are you harboring unforgiveness against anyone in your family for doing any of the following things to you: For intentionally injuring you, for verbally abusing you, for falsely accusing you, for abandoning you, for not protecting you, for betraying an intimate trust, or for sexually violating you (i.e. abuse, rape, touching, or looking)?

Are you harboring unforgiveness against yourself for doing any of the following things: For participating in the taking of life (abortion, counseling someone else to get an abortion, murder, assisting in a suicide), for injuring someone, for sexually violating someone, for being sexually violated, or for injuring the person of Jesus Christ?

Are you blaming God, and therefore harboring unforgiveness against Him, for doing any of the following things: For extreme sickness or disease in your life or in the life of someone else, for the death of someone close to you, for extreme challenges you may have faced in life, or for the verbal, physical, or sexual abuse inflicted on you or someone else close to you?

Inordinate Affections

If someone you knew was consumed with ham, you might think them a bit strange. If they always thought about ham, sang songs about ham, read books about ham, watched shows about ham, and then every time you were around them they talked about ham, you may conclude that they have an inordinate affection for ham. Ham, in and of itself, is a harmless thing. Yet when it occupies someone's mind to an unhealthy degree, it becomes harmful to the sacred sanctuary of an individual. Inordinate affections usually surface when you lie down in bed at night. If, when you lie down, your mind always goes to the same old subject, then it's very possible that you have an inordinate affection toward that subject. The sacred sanctuary is the place where God designed your affections to be centered. He intended that you would find complete satisfaction in knowing, loving, and adoring Him. Whenever something else captures your heart and your affections, it draws you very subtly out of your intimate relationship with Christ. Therefore, inordinate affections must be removed. After all, the first commandment given to Moses was, "You should be no other gods before Me" (Ex. 20:3). Nothing should ever be allowed to block your worship, love, and adoration from being fully expressed to your Heavenly Prince.

Recognizing Inordinate Affections

If you answer yes to any of the seven following questions then carefully walk through steps 1, 2, and 3 of the "Five Steps to Freedom" process found on pages 126-127. When you pray both individually and with your Christian teammate ask the Holy Spirit to powerfully break the unhealthy and controlling hold that the inordinate affection has over your mind. The key to freedom from inordinate affections is to first recognize that they are there. Then it becomes much easier to notice them, and therefore, fight them more effectively from this day forward.

Do you find that your mind spends far too much of its focus on any of the following: On your outward appearance? On your physical health? On what other people think about you? On things you said or did? On being current with the most recent trends for dress, talk, and behavior?

Do you find that your mind spends its focus on any of the following: On looking for things that are wrong with others? On comparing yourself with the way others talk, dress, look, or behave? On looking for things that are wrong with you or with your life?

Do you find that your mind is enslaved to focusing on the opposite sex in an unhealthy way? On pondering the opposite sex for unhealthy amounts of time? On wondering if you are liked by certain members of the opposite sex? On imagining you and certain members of the opposite sex together as an intimate couple? On imagining certain members of the opposite sex in a sexually explicit manner?

Do you find that your mind spends far too much of its focus on any of the following: Your personal success in some venture (a game, a competition, a performance, the taking of a test, the finishing of a project, etc.)? Someone else's success in some venture (a game, a competition, a performance, the taking of a test, the finishing of a project, etc.)?

Do you find that your mind is enslaved to focus on any of the following: On things that are imaginary? On things that could be, but aren't? On what could have been, but isn't? On things that have never happened, but could? On things that did happen that you wish hadn't?

Do you find that your mind is enslaved to focus on things that bring you personal comfort: (i.e. sexual closeness, drugs, alcohol, nicotine, gossip, music, money, sports, movies, clothing, shopping, etc.)

Do you find that your mind is enslaved to focus on things that are harmful to you and/or to others: (i.e. violence to others or inflicting violence on yourself?) If yes, then please confide in your Christian teammate and a biblical counselor as soon as possible so that you can more intimately work through the removal of this inordinate affection.

Ungodly Allurements

Ungodly allurements are a young soul's poison. If the soul were to be likened to a young puppy, then ungodly allurements would be like chicken bones. Little puppies are extremely attracted to both the smell and the taste of a chicken bone, but a chicken bone can be very dangerous, even deadly. Ungodly allurements are extremely attractive to us as humans, but equally as dangerous to our sacred sanctuary. Ungodly allurements, if allowed into the life of a Christian, choke out the presence of Christ over time, convincing us that building our lives completely around Christ is foolishness. Ungodly allurements are things that we allow into our lives to entertain us, inform us, and bring comfort to us. But if these forms of entertainment, information, and comfort are contrary to the nature of Christ, they must be handled very carefully. When you were two years old, your parents told you to never touch the stove, not because the stove was a bad thing, but because as a two-year-old you weren't ready yet to know how to make it a useful instrument. As a two-year-old, a stove represented only one thing — a very bad burn!

Ungodly allurements are somewhat similar. After many years of maturing as a Christian in an intimate love relationship with your Prince, it is possible to utilize these "allurements" as tools in your hand to help you more effectively reach the world around you for Christ. However, most of us are little puppies choking on the chicken bones. We are little toddlers who need to stay away from the stove until we are mature enough to make it useful to our lives. An ungodly allurement can be transformed into a godly tool only when your mind has been rebuilt by the Spirit of God. At that point, no longer do you look to this input as a means of understanding what to believe, but look to this input as a means of understanding how others are trained to believe and how to possibly reach them.

Recognizing Ungodly Allurements

Look over the following list of potential "allurements." Ask the Spirit of God to show you if any of these inputs or entertainment devices have been an unhealthy influence upon your sacred sanctuary with your Prince. If so, then carefully walk through steps 1, 2, and 3 of the "Five Steps to Freedom" process detailed on pages 126-127.

Potential Allurements

Television — Have you allowed television to negatively influence your behavior, thinking patterns, sense of right and wrong, or your attitude towards God, life, and/or others?

Movies – Have you allowed movies to negatively influence your behavior, thinking patterns, sense of right and wrong, or your attitude towards God, life, and/or others?

Music – Have you allowed music to negatively influence your behavior, thinking patterns, sense of right and wrong, or your attitude towards God, life, and/or others?

Books – Have you allowed books to negatively influence your behavior, thinking patterns, sense of right and wrong, or your attitude towards God, life, and/or others?

Magazines – Have you allowed magazines to negatively influence your behavior, thinking patterns, sense of right and wrong, or your attitude towards God, life, and/or others?

Newspapers – Have you allowed newspapers to negatively influence your behavior, thinking patterns, sense of right and wrong, or your attitude towards God, life, and/or others?

Internet – Have you allowed your activities on the internet to negatively influence your behavior, thinking patterns, sense of right and wrong, or your attitude towards God, life, and/or others?

Friends – Have you allowed certain friendships in your life to negatively influence your behavior, thinking patterns, sense of right and wrong, or your attitude towards God, life, and/or others?

Admirable People – Have you allowed certain people that you admire to negatively influence your behavior, thinking patterns, sense of right and wrong, or your attitude towards God, life, and/or others?

Romantic Relationships – Have you allowed certain romantic relationships in your life to negatively influence your behavior, thinking patterns, sense of right and wrong, or your attitude towards God, life, and/or others?

Cultural Norms — Have you allowed certain cultural norms (activities and behaviors that are acceptable to society — i.e. materialism, workaholism, premarital sexual activity, etc.) to negatively influence your behavior, thinking patterns, sense of right and wrong, or your attitude towards God, life, and/or others?

Final Thoughts

Please keep in mind that the above guidelines are not a conclusive list of sins. Ask God's Holy Spirit to guide you throughout this process and bring to mind issues in your life that may not have been included in the above material. It is also important to be aware that this house-cleaning process is not just a one-time effort; we must give continual attention to the ongoing process of keeping our inner sanctuary swept clean for our Prince. I highly recommend going through an internal examination processes like the one above repeatedly throughout your life.

Notes

Week One: Set-Apartness Defined

1. Charles Spurgeon, "A Sermon for Spring," No. 436, February 23, 1862, http://www.ccel.org/ccel/spurgeon/sermons08.x.html
2. Amy Carmichael, *God's Missionary* (Fort Washington: CLC, 1997).

Week Two: Surrender – Daring to Lay Everything Down at Jesus' Feet

1. V. Raymond Edman, *They Found the Secret* (New York City: Harper Collins, 1984), 152-158.
2. Amy Carmichael, *Gold Cord* (Fort Washington: CLC, 2002).
3. Elisabeth Elliot, *Shadow of the Almighty* (Peabody: Hendrickson, 2008), 74.
4. Reidhead, Paris. "Ten Shekels and a Shirt." Audio Sermon. http://www.sermonindex.net/modules/mydownloads/singlefile.php?lid=282&commentView=itemComments
5. Francis Ridley Havergal. "Take My Life, and Let It Be." 1874.

Week Three: Freedom – Allowing the Gospel to Transform You from the Inside Out

1. Source unknown.
2. Elisabeth Elliot, *Discipline: The Glad Surrender* (Grand Rapids: Revell, 2006),142.
3. Edith Deen, *Great Women of the Christin Faith* (Uhrichsville: Barbour Publishing, Inc., 1986), 223.
4. Corrie ten Boom, "Corrie ten Boom," AZ Quotes: Wind and Fly LTD, 2019. 1 June 2019. https://www.azquotes.com/quote/423874
5. Evan Hopkins, *The Law of Liberty in the Spiritual Life* (London: Marshall Brothers, 1884), 127-128.
6. Andrew Bonar, *The Biography of Robert Murray M'Cheyne* (Hamburg: Tredition, 2012).

Week Four: Intimacy – Cultivating Daily, Passionate Communion with Christ

1. A.W. Tozer, *God's Pursuit of Man* (Chicago: Moody, 2015).
2. Corrie ten Boom, "Corrie ten Boom," AZ Quotes: Wind and Fly LTD, 2019. 1 June 2019. https://www.azquotes.com/quote/519578.
3. Elisabeth Elliot, *Discipline: The Glad Surrender* (Grand Rapids: Revell, 2006), 104.
4. E.G. Carré, *Praying Hyde: Apostle of Prayer: The Life Story of John Hyde* (Alachua: Bridge-Logos, 2004), 129.
5. Amy Carmichael, *His Thoughts Said… His Father Said…* (Fort Washington: CLC, 2012), 10.
6. Leonard Ravenhill, *Why Revival Tarries* (Minneapolis: Bethany House, 2004), 85.

Week Five: Devotion – Fixing Your Gaze Completely on Jesus

1. C.T. Studd, *Cricketer and Pioneer* (Cambridge: Lutterworth Press, 2014).
2. Lilias Trotter, "Our Inspiration," The Lilias Trotter Center, 2016: https://www.liliastrottercenter.org/lilias-trotter-1
3. Amy Carmichael, *God's Missionary* (Fort Washington: CLC, 1998), 32-33.
4. Lilias Trotter, "Our Inspiration," The Lilias Trotter Center, 2016: https://www.liliastrottercenter.org/lilias-trotter-1

Week Six: Radiance – Overcoming Insecurity through the Crucified Life

1. Leslie Ludy, *Set Apart Femininity* (Eugene: Harvest House, 2008), 46.
2. Source unknown.
3. "Elisabeth Elliot." AZQuotes.com. Wind and Fly LTD, 2019. 07 June 2019. https://www.azquotes.com/quote/486054
4. Source unknown.
5. Amy Carmichael, *If: What Do I Know of Calvary Love?* (Fort Washington: CLC, 1992).
6. Amy Carmichael, *Gold Cord: The Story of a Fellowship* (London: Society for Promoting Christian Knowledge, 1952), 40.

Week Eight: Nobility – Honoring God and Others with Every Word Spoken

1. Amy Carmichael, *If: What Do I Know of Calvary Love?* (Fort Washington: CLC, 1992).
2. Amy Carmichael, *Gold Cord* (Fort Washington: CLC, 1999), 67–68.

Week Nine: Friendship – Becoming a Faithful "Friend of the Bridegroom"

1. Amy Carmichael, *If: What Do I Know of Calvary Love?* (Fort Washington: CLC, 1992).
2. Amy Carmichael, *Thou Givest, They Gather* (Fort Washington: CLC, 2003).
3. "Elisabeth Elliot." AZQuotes.com. Wind and Fly LTD, 2019. 01 June 2019. https://www.azquotes.com/quote/486054

Week Ten: Discernment – Overcoming Deception through Godly Wisdom

1. Corrie ten Boom, *The Hiding Place* (Grand Rapids: Chosen Books, 2006), 173.
2. Catherine Booth, *Aggressive Christianity: Practical Sermons* (Philadelphia: National Publishing Association for the Promotion of Holiness, 1883), 32.

Week Eleven: Courage – Becoming Fearless for Such a Time as This

1. "Martin Luther." AZQuotes.com. Wind and Fly LTD, 2019. 1 June 2019. https://www.azquotes.com/quote/579401
2. L.B. Cowman, *Streams in the Desert* (Grand Rapids: Zondervan, 1996), 221.
3. James Gilmour, James Gilmour of Mongolia: His Diaries, Letters, and Reports (Mongolia: Religious Tract Society, 1892), 52.

Week Twelve: Love – Discovering the Power of a Poured-Out Life

1. Edith Deen, Great Women of the Christian Faith (Westwood: Barbour, 1959), 220.
2. William Booth, *The General's Letters, 1885* (London: The Salvation Army, 1885), 4.
3. Homepage: "Hunger and World Poverty," poverty.com: 2019. 1 June 2019. www.poverty.com
4. Unicef estimates that there are 153 million orphans in the world today.
5. USA Today: "There are 40 Million Slaves Worldwide, Most Are Women and Girls," USA Today: Sean Rossman, 2017. 4 April 2019.
6. Leslie Ludy, *Sacred Singleness* (Eugene: Harvest House, 2009), 152.
7. Thabiti Anyabwile, "105 People Die Each Minute," The Gospel Coalition: 2016. 1 September 2017. https://www.thegospelcoalition.org/article/105-people-die-each-minute
8. Miriam Huffman Rockness, A Passion for the Impossible: The Life of Lilias Trotter (Grand Rapids: Discovery House, 2014).
9. Amy Carmichael, *Candles in the Dark: Letters of Hope and Encouragement* (Fort Washington: CLC, 2010), 84 (paraphrased).

Printed in Great Britain
by Amazon